THE TECH
TRAP

THE TECH TRAP

A MOM'S FIGHT FOR HER DAUGHTER IN A

WORLD OF MODERN TECHNOLOGY

DEBORAH BERRY

Cover Design: Rachel L. Berry

ISBN 13: 978-1-954020-14-6

14 15 16 17 18 19 10 9 8 7 6 5 4 3 2 1

First Edition

To my extraordinarily brave daughter, who is greatly loved.

*You have risen to the occasion and in the process
made me a better mother.*

Acknowledgments

With love and gratitude to my husband and children who walk this continued journey with me. Your unwavering love and encouragement remain the driving force behind my ability to express myself through the written word.

To my wonderful mom who always had words of encouragement and more than a minute to listen to me read the latest addition. You are my best friend and I have learned so much from you. Your spiritual guidance has been a difference maker in how I live my life.

To my one-of-a-kind dad who spent many hours listening to me throughout this process and who greatly encouraged me to give my all to the story and fully own the content of the book. Your unique perspective enriched my point of view.

To my awesome brother, Robert, who believed in my ability to write from minute one. Your confidence in me means more than you will ever know. Thank you for helping me out of the starting gate.

To my amazing sister, Sharon, who is ready and willing to help me take my vision to the next level, thank you for all that you selflessly do.

With heartfelt thanks to Bobby Nix who welcomed my project with open arms and great enthusiasm. Your support and dedication in helping smooth out the rough edges has made all the difference. And to his wife, Trina, who provided valuable feedback. You are the best!

Jane Samuel, you are a gentle nurturer who planted the seed and encouraged the research which led to the writing of this book. Your insight provided me with much to think about and I am so grateful.

With great affection for Angie Fusco, whom I greatly respect for her boldness and honesty. You were always willing to take my phone calls and answer my endless questions. Thank you, friend!

Special thanks to Allen Cardoza who was willing to share his extensive knowledge with me. Your kindness and generosity with your time and resources are very much appreciated.

With sincere thanks to certain members of the law enforcement community for your passion in making our world a better and safer place for our children. The material you shared was invaluable.

Contents

Part Three: The Resources

Letter from My Daughter

I boarded the plane at seven o'clock am to unknowingly start a new life. I was in transit from the bustling city of Houston, TX to the serene Blue Ridge Mountains of North Carolina to enroll in a therapeutic wilderness program. This was my parent's choice to send me there however, my actions and behavior were begging for them to take action.

I was twelve years old and on the verge of being sex trafficked. I had been hiding my secret life from my parents for two years until a random phone check performed by my mom revealed any parent's nightmare. My parents knew that in order to keep me safe they would have to send me away and strip me of any contact from the outside world.

My last words before leaving my parents were harsh and quick. " I wish you would have told me this was going to happen two years ago." I turned to walk away depriving them of a goodbye or hug. I was then driven away for what felt like the longest thirty minutes of my life. I spent the car ride quietly crying, trying to keep any weakness or emotion to myself. And with nothing of my own possession, I entered the wilderness.

I slowly adapted to living in the woods, however I quickly learned things such as how to start a fire in a primitive manner called bowdrilling, and how to stay safe during a thunderstorm while trees snapped around me. I learned how to create a temporary shelter with a plastic tarp that provided little protection from anything but the rain above. I slept every night listening to the coyotes howl in the distance and would wake up to fresh bear scat surrounding our campground.

Three months in the wilderness turned into four years at different boarding schools. After being away for so long the end or way out felt no longer visible. About the second year away, and second boarding school. I stopped fighting and just accepted that I was in treatment and the only way out was to do what I was supposed to do.

Being away from home was hard, I had to grow up and spend most of my teenage years without seeing my parents but once every two months. Going into it I had no clue what I was capable of, but there was no better way of finding myself than the way I did. I am grateful for being pulled away from my old life and redirected into a new one, one that has taught me so many life lessons.

I boarded the plane at seven o'clock a.m. to unknowingly start a new life. I was in transit from the bustling city of Houston, Texas to the serene Blue Ridge Mountains of North Carolina to enroll in a therapeutic wilderness program. This was my parent's choice to send me there; however, my actions and behavior were begging for them to take action.

I was twelve years old and on the verge of being sex trafficked. I had been hiding my secret life from my parents for two years until a random phone check performed by my mom revealed any parent's nightmare.

My parents knew that in order to keep me safe they would have to send me away and strip me of any contact from the outside world.

My last words before leaving my parents were harsh and quick, "I wish you would have told me this was going to happen two years ago." I turned to walk away depriving them of a goodbye or hug.

I was then driven away for what felt like the longest thirty minutes of my life. I spent the car ride quietly crying, trying to keep any weakness or emotion to myself. And with nothing of my own possession, I entered the wilderness.

I slowly adapted to living in the woods; however, I quickly learned things such as how to start a fire in a primitive manner called bow-drilling, and how to stay safe during a thunderstorm while trees snapped around me. I learned how to create a temporary shelter with a plastic tarp that provided little protection from anything but the rain above. I slept every night listening to the coyotes howl in the distance and would wake up to fresh bear scat surrounding our campground.

Three months in the wilderness turned into four years at different boarding schools. After being away for so long, the end or way out felt no longer visible. About the second year away, and second boarding school, I stopped fighting and just accepted that I was in treatment and the only way out was to do what I was supposed to do.

Being away from home was hard. I had to grow up and spend most of my teenage years without seeing my parents but once every two months. Going into it, I had no clue what I was capable of, but there was no better way of finding myself than the way I did. I am grateful for being pulled away from my old life and redirected into a new one, one that has taught me so many life lessons.

Author's Note

The words on the pages that follow were written unguarded and with truth as I authentically experienced it. It is a story of a mother's perspective on what happened to her very young daughter in a world filled with technology. It is an account of the action taken in hopes of changing the dangerous road her vulnerable daughter started to walk down.

Upon the shocking discovery of the virtual world my daughter was living in, a series of decisions were set into motion, resulting in a four-year journey that included living in the wilderness and attending several therapeutic boarding schools until eventually she returned home.

The catalyst for this cautionary tale began as an effort to educate myself and my daughter regarding the world of social media before leaving the protection of a tech-free boarding school. My research efforts turned into a desire to share the information I discovered along the way.

Untold numbers of families are suffering in silent distress as they attempt to navigate unknown waters for their children in crisis. It is my hope that by sharing my personal journey, I will provide light and encouragement along the way.

PART ONE

The Journey

One

Revelations from the Journey

There is a world before the Wilderness and Therapeutic Boarding School and there is a world after.

The world before is the one that we all strive for. Precisely coordinated carpools. Savory crock-pot meals between sports practices and homework. Girl Scout cookies, summer camp, and church on Sunday.

The world after is the one that is full of judgment. It is unfamiliar and feels like the wild frontier. There is no map, no clear-cut directions. It is a very confusing, dark, and lonely place full of desperation. There are no friends, there is no support, and shame is your companion.

Cautious parents subtly move in a direction opposite of you and your child. The party invitation is perpetually lost in the mail. There is an uneasy awareness; instinctively you know you are being talked about behind your back.

And so it goes. We made our exit at the end of sixth

grade and no one even noticed we did not return in the fall. In short order, I found myself in the registrar's office of the middle school withdrawing my daughter. The process left me feeling exposed and uncomfortable as if I had done something wrong. As I unraveled the tentacles tethering her to a traditional education, I knew her broken pieces could never be put back together in the same way. I held my new mantra as if it were a shield of armor . . . "Don't look back, we're not going that way."

Decisions needed to be made. I could project a few short years into the future and imagine the worst in addictions, promiscuity, and a lost life full of lies. Where there is smoke, there is fire, and it was only a matter of time before my house was burning down. I was obsessed with making the right decision, turning the details over again and again in my mind. I prayed for guidance to help me get it right the first time. It was imperative in order for me to live with myself.

Parenting was the holy grail for me, and I could not and would not live with regret. At the end of the day, she remained ultimately responsible for her choices, but I needed to know I had done everything within my power to provide her with love and unwavering support. I needed her to know I had her back and would crawl across broken glass for her. At the same time, I believed in the wisdom of letting those you love take their destined journey. My interference in that process would cheat her out of the lessons and life she was intended to live.

I wrestled with my competence to parent. I had devoted my life to my children and suddenly found myself in uncharted territory, out of answers. I was raw with emotion knowing this child stripped me of my ability to cope and what was worse, I felt it in every bone of my body. I was not detached and I was exhausted. I hated the morning dawn, knowing it would only bring another day that looked exactly like yesterday. She was full of defiance, disrespect, and hate, yet my daughter was only a child. I mused that God would never take me because that would be too easy.

To lay my head down on a pillow, close my eyes and not awaken to this Earth was an enticing thought. Gone would be the pain and heartache of the struggle—in its place would be sweet relief washing over me, making me feel whole again. A permanent solution which was no real solution at all. I would remain and honor the agreement I had made, relying on every ounce of courage I had to move myself forward.

The idea of turning my child over to others to do what I had not been able to cut me to my absolute core. You may as well have reached in and pulled my heart out. Painfully exposed, I reconciled the truth as I knew it: I had to check my mother ego. It was less selfish of me to let go than it was of me to hold on. The few short years taken in order to heal would be worth the next sixty in health. God willing.

More than once, I endlessly questioned the professionals; "Did it take a sledgehammer to kill a mosquito?" Well, the answer was yes. The best results require foresight. Quick action equates to time, and time equates to options. Control of what happens and how it happens is in the hands of the parent until the age of eighteen. That is a very powerful insight. There was something deep inside me that intuitively knew this was correct. It was time to cross over.

The Wilderness* offered light where there was darkness. There was hope to reset where no one cares who your family is or where you came from. It is about being quietly still without distractions. Nature holds no judgment; it only demands you cooperate or face consequences. It was a perfect untainted environment in which to reconnect to the core of what it means to be purely human. Living in the wilderness would make her different. We had stepped off the traditional path. It would be unpredictable from this point forward—we did not know where this road would lead.

There would be no return to normal, rather it was a new normal. I was comfortable in my own skin and never worried too much about what others thought. But this was different, this was my child. I wanted to protect her from the cruel whispers of society. I warned her to keep her story to herself in the event she returned to school. No one should know her dark secrets, as they would surely be used against her.

I spent a lot of time blaming myself, two years to be

---

*A Wilderness Therapy Program is a specialized outdoor experience designed to assess, clearly diagnose, and deal with behavioral issues leading to recommendations for the next level of care.

exact. I felt certain I had failed my daughter somewhere along the way. With surgical precision, I played the "what if" game in my dreams at night knowing I held the ultimate responsibility for her well-being. What had I done, what had I failed to do? I turned over every stone and looked around every corner searching for the moment I wish I could take back.

One day I decided maybe this was not about me. Just maybe it was about her. Was it possible I had been chosen to help her navigate her destined path through life? Just maybe God thought highly enough of me to grant me the task of loving her unconditionally on this journey.

Eventually I settled down, knowing the answers would be provided to me at the exact moment I needed them the most. I learned to trust myself and listen for God in this partnership. Admittedly, I did not always understand, and would question why. Every now and again my emotions would get the better of me and I would become filled with anger, frustration, resentment, and overwhelming sadness. When that happened, circumstances would carry me along to the next step whether I wanted to go or not.

In my quiet moments of reflection, I could recognize God's handiwork, which often left me amazed at the perfect synchronicity of His universe. Nothing was left to waste and that was stunningly awesome. I once again felt gratitude to be a part of His miracle as I continued on this path with my daughter.

Two

The Tech Trap

Do not get me wrong, I love my technology. Just this morning I used Google Maps to get to my appointment, order a book off of Amazon, and make dinner reservations, all before noon. Later, I surfed the web, researching ideas for our next family vacation. In between looking at flights and hotels, I sent a family group text, warning of inclement weather . . . which I checked on my weather app.

However, I did not love technology so much on a spring day in 2016. My world as I had known it instantly and permanently changed. Before the end of the day, I would be irreversibly plunged into crisis management mode, making decisions I never thought I would need to make.

It was an ordinary afternoon, and as was my habit, I monitored my youngest child's social media, making a mental note to be more consistent. On autopilot, I spot-checked the usual: Instagram, emails, and texts. All were clear. Then I did something I did not usually do, I looked at her photo library. They were typical photos a young middle schooler would take: silly faces, funny poses, and awkward attempts to appear cool and more grown up than the reality of the sheltered twelve years she had already lived. Amused, I continued to work my way backward, until unexpectedly I came across a series of screenshots. Upon closer investigation, I was alarmed to realize the text exchanges were between random strangers and my daughter.

Like a deer in the headlights, I became paralyzed as chills ran over my body. Unable to comprehend, I slowly and deliberately re-read each text exchange, trying to process indelicate language while keeping my composure. As my gut churned, I instinctively knew this child was in over her head.

In that moment, I set forth on a journey I was stunned to find myself on. I would enter into a world I knew nothing of and wanted nothing to do with. I would deeply and painfully question my parenthood. I would wrestle endlessly with life-altering decisions. I would be brought to my knees, praying nightly to God to not create further wounds for this child. And along the way, I would learn to trust myself in this process.

I was undeniably headed for disaster. I could see the future by reading the handwriting on the wall; my beautiful twelve-year-old daughter would eventually look me in the eyes and say, "Fuck you." I would not recognize her shameless disrespect, foul language, flippant attitude, or sexualized behavior. That moment came sooner than I thought. Waves of trepidation washed over me as I tried to decipher the eerie feeling deep inside the pit of my stomach that left me feeling nauseous. As I watched my daughter rapidly transform before my eyes, I needed to ascertain who and what I was dealing with.

The screenshots I found that spring day strongly suggested I had only stumbled across the tip of the iceberg. Ultimately her computer would hold the key. If I could only figure out how to resurrect her past. Intuitively, I knew as most mothers do, there would be collateral damage in what I found. With total resolve, I nervously implored my older daughter to comb the history, temp files, and cookies associated with the computer in question. We braced ourselves as she dug deep, eventually locating and unearthing the evidence of her sister's covert activities. It was a total gut punch. I felt sick to my stomach while my heart shattered. Free-falling with nothing to hold on to, I struggled to calm myself.

In complete horror, I witnessed a history of countless visits to vile adult porn sites, interactions with sleazy dating sites, and personal screenshot images that were difficult to look at. Was that my daughter? Red flags from the past began to stitch themselves together as the world crashed around me and landed squarely on my shoulders. In that instant, life as I knew it took a hard pivot.

What was I going to do? I do not know why, but I felt a heightened sense of urgency to take action as if her life depended on it. Later, my suspicions would be confirmed as I would discover she had a failed attempt to meet with one of her predators who had been masquerading as a boyfriend. As the gravity of the situation set in, I realized in that moment, my daughter could have been the next innocent young girl on a sex trafficker's auction block never to be seen or heard from again or the newest pre-teen addition to an online pornographic catalogue for perverts. We had dodged a bullet; in fact, I believed we saved her life, although I will never know for certain. It would be several more years before I would learn more specifics of the traumatizing truth; the sketchy details of the journey a cyber sexual predator took her on starting at the vulnerable age of ten.

It was during this uncertain period of time I ran into a friend I had known for many years, but had not seen for quite some time. This particular friend always seemed to randomly surface when I needed information and direction. True to form, over a casual lunch, she quickly launched into a personal story regarding the troubles of one of her children and subsequent placement in a specialized program. She had identified the program through the guidance of a professional service. It was as if she had read my mind. A deep wave of relief washed over me as I realized she was providing me with information for a path forward. This was the first time I had heard of Educational Consultants.

Ed consultants, as they are commonly called, specialize in accessing unique needs and circumstances of kids and matching them to an identified program. That was the very thing I needed, someone to provide direction and options. I was fighting with my daughter, wrangling with my emotions, and battling my overwhelming disappointment. I needed a lifeline. I needed a plan.

At twelve years of age, my bold and fiery daughter entered the Nantahala Mountain wilderness for a duration of ninety endless days and nights. The wilderness was followed by a two-year stint in a therapeutic boarding school for pre-teen girls, followed by eighteen months in yet another therapeutic boarding school located in the North Carolina countryside. It was a very long four years.

I am eternally grateful to the professionals who kept my daughter safe from the unforgiving world of social media and the many life-altering consequences that potentially follow. She is beyond fortunate. At the same time, I slowly came to the realization my daughter was essentially placed on technological ice and I knew this would not last forever. She would return home and as much as I wanted to, there was no putting the tech genie back into the bottle.

My fears and concerns surrounding social media and all things internet remained unaddressed. I was scared. The dedicated therapists, who work tirelessly, simply had not caught up with the rapidly changing underworld of dark tech. I was not convinced my daughter fully understood internet dangers and could very likely return to high-risk behavior. I was not about to roll the dice. Desperate, I turned to my parent coach, who often was my stabilizer and lifeline. She encouraged me to pursue my concerns and press the issue with my daughter's therapist. I resolved to take matters into my own hands, do the research, and educate myself and my daughter before she left the safety of the tech-free boarding school and returned home. I reasoned, at the very least, she would make poor but educated decisions. So, with that in mind, I began the research that would shock me and forever change the way I view technology in our society. I would like to share my journey with you.

Three

Weighing the Options

Behind a closed door late at night, I scoured the internet searching for insight and direction in an attempt to formulate a plan for my daughter.

Typing the key words: *programs*, *teens and social media*, *life skills*, and *technology abuse* relentlessly into my computer; I implored the internet to produce the answers. Decidedly, the effort only resulted in spewing out a cocktail of endless possibilities leaving me in a tailspin. Discouraged, I slammed my laptop closed while I tightly squeezed my eyes shut and willed it all to go away. In anger, I sobbed aloud, "Why would God give me a child I was so ill-equipped to handle?" No one answered back.

Looking for alternatives, my thoughts remained disjointed. Should I soft-serve or hard-serve this child? How far would I need to go in order to gain her attention? She was playing a dangerous game she was convinced she un-

derstood and was in control of. As was my natural inclination, I wanted to be the gentle teacher, but as I already
knew from experience, she was a strong-willed kid who
was more inclined to learn the hard way. Was I getting in
front of this situation or was I already behind it? Should
I wait for something more concrete to justify my actions;
after all, she was only twelve years old and a victim. She
had suffered trauma. It was not like she had run away,
been drinking, or taking drugs. Would I cause more damage sending her away or was I saving her from future suffering? I was gambling with my daughter's life and I was
not about to lose.

I talked myself into and out of possible solutions, vac-
illating between numerous scenarios. Where was the protocol that would allow me to plug in her symptoms and
produce a remedy? Where were the damn answers?

Upon landing on a website for youth programs, I would
quickly scroll down to the reviews and read anything from
"they saved my child's life" to "this program is the worst
thing you could ever do to your kid." So, which was it and
how would I know? The truth is, you do not know.

What I did know at this juncture in our lives was an
undeniable fork in the road had emerged. My daughter's
behavior was steadily ramping up. She was now reject-
ing hugs from my husband, telling him he was not her
father, and to leave her alone. She was now spontaneously
flicking water from a straw into my face and muttering
"screw you" under her breath. She was now jerking away
from my parental hold and seething while telling me to get

my hands off of her. She was unable to grow through the out-of-control screaming tantrums of a three-year-old child and would not allow me or others to connect with her. She was living like an enraged animal in a perpetual state of defense, prepared to attack anything that crossed her path.

Her temperament had been difficult from an early age and throughout the years she had increasingly become a disciplinarian challenge. Unbeknownst to me, a sequence of events had already been placed in motion that would lead her into the technological weeds of the dark internet. The connection would set fire to her occasional deviance rendering such behavior no longer the exception to the rule, but rather a habitual norm. As a result, starting around the age of ten, I had threatened her on and off multiple times with extreme discipline found in boarding schools. Her father had threatened military school. The person I had become in order to consistently discipline her was someone I was starting to abhor. I hated who I was turning into and it was rapidly destroying me. My back was against the wall and something needed to give. The days of empty threats were quickly coming to an end and it was time to calm the whirlwind of chaos inside her. The conflicting messages from the complex world she lived in would need to be addressed in order for her to make sense of her struggles.

Having exhausted my resources, I finally arrived at the conclusion I needed professional help to determine a course of action and sort through the endless rabbit trails I had been running down. The educational consultant would require pages of paperwork documenting my daughter's tormented history. Next, there would be more contractual paperwork cementing our financial agreement. Upon completion, she would meet with me (and eventually my daughter) to assimilate the information and make recommendations. After client placement, the contract promised bi-weekly communications on my behalf between the educational consultant and the program. This was done with the intention of tracking my daughter's progress in preparation for the post-program placement. *What post-program placement?* I brushed it aside as I could only digest one step at a time.

In short order, I was provided a printed report listing twelve different options and attached program descriptions. The list covered the gamut, including structured summer camp, state programs, and wilderness programs. That was it. Apparently, it was my job to figure out which program and let the educational consultant know.

I quickly eliminated the traditional summer camp programs; we had been there, done that. The state programs were mired down in requirements and did not appear to provide the safety and customized attention I was looking for. This left the wilderness option, which reasoned out to be the most impactful. It was the tough love she needed and it would rip her world away and turn it upside down. If I was going to shoot an arrow, I intended to hit the target.

It was the most painful and difficult decision my husband and I would make. My daughter's actions had scared the living hell out of me. Honestly, I felt like I had failed as her mother. I wondered if I had done enough, talked enough, loved her enough. Being her mother was so important to me and I was distraught to realize I had not done something right. I was tortured by the very thought. I believed if I sent her to the wilderness, I would be giving up on her, passing my responsibility to someone else because I could not handle it, while at the same time failing at my life's work. I was losing control and it was the most devastating feeling in the world. At the same time, I felt guilty for being relieved of her constant supervision. It would be nice to not endlessly worry about her and feel the weight of the world unceasingly beating down upon my shoulders. It would be good to close my eyes and breathe again. In the wilderness, I knew she would be safe from the actions of others as well as her own actions. There would be no way for any of the people she interfaced with to track her down. More importantly, there would be no way for her to attempt to meet them. Yes, wilderness was the right decision. She would be safe.

Remaining vigilant in my decision-making process, I contacted my daughter's psychiatrist and asked her to review the two possible wilderness programs. I relied on her professional expertise to evaluate the methodology of the programs. With her recommendation, we proceeded.

For the next four years my husband and I would hemorrhage money while healing our daughter. We were already suffering from sticker shock with a price tag of $6,000 for the educational consultant before we were even committed to a program. The wilderness programs cost an average of $500–600 per day for an average stay of seventy to ninety days. The state does not cover such programs, and insurance rarely covers little else other than billable therapy hours. Basically, you are on your own.

Would the wilderness resolve all the issues at hand? In our case, it was only the beginning. Wilderness would be followed by three-and-a-half years of therapeutic boarding school at a conservative rate of $8–10,000 per month.

The financial commitment cannot be understated; it was simply overwhelming and, in many instances, life altering. During the time my daughter was in treatment, I would learn of the selfless actions and great sacrifices many parents made on behalf of their daughters. In order to raise the necessary funds, it was not uncommon for the decision to be made to sell the family home, cash in a 401k and/or take out loans. I realize that not all families or single parents can take on this extreme financial burden, and that is okay. The information provided is just that— information that may help some people on this difficult journey.

Four

The Wilderness

The decision was made. I had one shot at this kid and I had to get it right the first time. She had become fiercely oppositional and more brazenly defiant by the day.

The moment the first layer of my daughter's double life became exposed, I attempted to address it. I tried to trick her, telling her I had found everything, when in fact I had not. I tried to psych her out, insisting I knew about all the things she had been up to. With a childlike face devoid of emotion, she insisted she did not know what I was talking about. She outright rejected and denied my onslaught of accusations, leaving no visible crack in her shield of armor. She held steady while I attempted to gain a foothold and knock her off center, but to no avail.

Long, sleepless nights left me alone with my thoughts as they weighed heavy on my heart. I wrestled with all the knowns and unknowns while an occasional wave of panic worked its way to the surface.

I needed to strike the right balance. The countermeasure could not fall short because I did not believe I would have another opportunity. At the same time, I was terrified of crushing her spirit and extinguishing the spark that made her special. Was I approaching a point of no return?

There was yet another thing, something I valued greatly. I did not want to destroy her love for me. I knew I was risking our relationship and there would be no guarantee as to how this would shake out. We were headed fast for the ditch and I was not sure if I could save it. I knew what I had to do, but I also knew there would be no turning back and I needed to be prepared for all possible outcomes. There would be no do-overs with the next series of decisions I would make.

On more than one occasion, my daughter questioned her place in our family. She was much younger than her siblings, and often held the belief she was a mistake and not really wanted. This could not have been farther from the truth; she was anything but an accidental blessing.

What she did not know was the promise I made myself the day I learned I was pregnant. God had blessed me with one more miracle. I would fully embrace every moment of the next nine months, as this would be the last child I would carry and welcome into the world. What she could not remember was the moment following her birth that took my breath away. As I gently held her in my arms for the first time, she opened her eyes and looked directly into mine, with all the vulnerability of a newborn. She intently held my gaze for what felt like all of time, yet no time at all. In that unexpected moment, it was not a mother and her newborn daughter, it was two beings knowingly looking into each other's souls. It was as if we recognized each other on another level; silently acknowledging a promise made long ago. Inherently I knew there was something very special about her and the life we would live together. I had no idea what lay in store, but in an eye blink, we were connected forever in an unbreakable bond. The moment quickly diminished into a memory as we settled in and quietly went about the business of being mother and daughter.

Like a warrior headed for battle, I prayed the following:

Dear God,

> *It is my intention to do right by this child as promised the day she was born. I am prepared to travel this unknown path. Lead me to the solution and I promise to recognize Your wisdom. Give me courage to accept Your answers whether I like them or not. Finally, I ask for continued strength to trust the process.*

I would repeat this prayer daily over the next four years as I fought to find my way.

As I had done so many times before, I laid down in bed beside her. In the familiar sanctuary of her quiet bedroom, I slowly turned to her. In a sedate voice, barely more than a whisper, I said to my daughter:

Life is not going so great for us right now. I am pretty miserable and I think you are too. You are unhappy and so am I. I didn't picture our life this way and it makes me really sad. I think we should do something about it. What if we could fix that? What if we could get these things worked out? Would it not be worth it? There is such a place called the Wilderness. It is where you go and camp for a while, sort of like Girl Scouts. You get to really know yourself; discover your strengths and grow as a person. It could be a reset for you. I think we have to try.

I did my best to sell her on the glossy brochure. I knew I had to get her to the program and her buy-in was crucial. On June 9, 2016, we boarded a plane for Atlanta, Georgia, and headed north toward a future we had no guarantee of.

The real brochure for the Wilderness painted a different picture. No cabins, no folding camp chairs, no toilets, no showers, and no cozy fireside chats. Upon arrival she would be stripped of all her worldly possessions including the city clothes on her back. She was issued wilderness clothing indistinguishable from the others. Her new uniform consisted of a pair of hiking boots, military type pants, and a long-sleeved khaki T-shirt. The regulation backpack was almost bigger than her tiny 5'2" frame, and I wondered if she would struggle to carry it on her back. The only item she would be allowed to keep was the faded pink bear-bear she had clung to since she was an infant. The worn stuffed animal with multicolored stitches would continue to be her faithful and silent companion.

I had prepared for an agonizing goodbye. Envisioning myself holding her and gently giving her a kiss, I knew I would have to look in her eyes and produce some confident words of reassurance; some compelling explanation as to why this was happening. The moment of dread was looming near as I discerned it was almost time. The staff asked if we would like a few moments alone out on the rustic, wooden porch to say our goodbyes. Hastily disregarding the invitation, my daughter abruptly spun around on her heels and with a rebellious tone said, "I wish you would have told me this was going to happen two years ago." Choking back my emotions I said, "I did." With that, she confidently countered, "Then let's get this done." She turned and walked away, quickly disappearing from sight. There was no hug, there was no kiss. That would be the last time I would see her for eighty days. I was devastated.

The pain inside was replaced with intermittent bouts of second-guessing my decision. I had just turned my daughter over to survivalists who held varying degrees in social work. They would be the only connection I had to her. There would be no phone calls, no weekend visits, no popping in to make sure all was okay. I would not even be made aware of her exact location in the woods. I had taken a leap of blind faith and it was the toughest love of all.

The subsequent days were filled with guilt. How could I enjoy myself while she was scared and alone? How could I climb into my clean warm bed at night while she slept on the hard ground? How could I laugh while she was crying? Worst of all, how could I wake up smiling and be happy when, in the back of my mind, I knew it was because I would not have to deal with her. In some ways, it was a relief to wake up without her.

At the same time, I was lost. The predictable routine I had lived for the past twenty years of my life revolved around my kids and now the last of them was suddenly gone. Overnight, the life work I had taken so much pride in was disrupted and furloughed until further notice. I had to walk away, leaving it in shambles. Essential strangers would now be her daily guardians. They would be the keepers of her secrets, witnesses to her victories, and the judge of her defeats. I would have to learn to live with it.

Live with it, I did. Despite my efforts to manage my new circumstances, it would not be long before I found myself caught off guard as I drove by the neighborhood school. Any other day, my daughter would have been among the carefree children I watched playing outside in the afternoon sun. Instead, she was a thousand miles away from home, and it crushed me in a way I was unprepared for. It was an odd feeling of deep displacement and sorrow, leaving me bitterly out of sorts. The glaring reality was I no longer belonged in the middle school carpool line, in the stands at the afternoon soccer games, or in the classroom on parents' night. My world had split without warning, and now I was headed in an unknown direction away from the predictable life of a middle school mother. I was not sure where I belonged, but I was sure I was alone.

Five

Into the Woods

We drove away from the field house in northern Georgia stunned and in disbelief. With each mile, the distance between us and our daughter grew wider. We had just signed over temporary guardianship of the child I had promised to protect at all costs. It felt unnatural and surreal. I had relinquished control and admitted defeat. With little more than blind faith, I agreed to step aside and entrust professionals to build a new foundation for the future of my daughter; something I had been unable to do.

Later that afternoon, they would transport her across the state line into North Carolina and head deep into the woods to a remote camp site. Before joining the coed group of seven kids, she would be required to sit apart from them in silent isolation for twenty-four hours. She had to earn her way into the group.

Terrified I would miss the first call from the Wilderness

program, I clung to my cell phone as if it were a lifeline. I could do little else as I counted the passing minutes, watching them turn into hours. Eventually I would have word from the therapist that she had transitioned well. I breathed a temporary sigh of relief.

The following is an excerpt from the impact letter I wrote to my daughter shortly after her arrival in the wilderness at age twelve.

Dear Daughter,

These last several years have been extremely difficult on you as well as me. I have parented you to the best of my ability and now feel there is no other choice but to send you to the wilderness where you will have a chance to discover who you are and who you want to be in this world. Perhaps most importantly, who you want to be in our family.

I feel very confident this will be a positive direction for you. I know you are probably very angry with us and that is okay. The truth of the matter is, this is a tremendous gift to you. Someday, I hope you understand. I want you to know that it is because of our love for you that we have made this decision. I believe you deserve better than what you have chosen to give yourself.

I truly believed you understood the danger in interacting with someone on social media who you did not know. Initially, all I could think of was the immediate danger you put yourself in. I panicked at the thought you could easily be picked up and taken from me. The things I know are possible in this world are so horrifying that I would not be able to live with that.

It is my hope you will discover the wonderful strengths you have as a person and learn to use them in a positive manner. I can only imagine the incredible possibilities you will have once you have successfully harnessed this energy.

Please remember, you always have the power of choice. You have more control over your life than you currently understand.

One last thought.

This is what I do know:

I love you, but I cannot do the work for you.

I love you, but I cannot want this more for you than you want it for yourself.

I love you, but you have to love yourself.

I do love you,

Mom

As the long summer days passed, my imagination remained unbridled and continued to run wild; at the same time there were intermittent moments of lucid rationale. While I baked in the Texas heat, I wondered how she managed life outdoors. As if I could control the elements, I obsessively checked the weather, imagining what conditions she was contending with. How did she manage during the summer pop-up thunderstorms? The ones that were so powerful they rattled windows and blinded you with flashes of lightning. With no permanent shelter, how did she negotiate endless days of rain? Was she safe? Was she scared? Did she want to live or did she want to die? Did she cry for her mother?

received June 23, 2016

Dear mom & Dad,

Camp is fun at times but its really hard to stay positive when I havent pooped in 1 week and having to sleep on 1/2 an inch pad everynight. Anyways the took everything away from me, accept bear bear. They provided me with a note pad, pen, packetwork, and a big pack of survival needs. everyone is really nice and welcoming, but I made a connection with Izzy. she's been here for two weeks, from Boulder, CO, 14 years old. She's here from another facility and got transferred. Her parents sent her here because of drugs & achohol. running away too. But overall shes really, really, nice & funny.

I also recieved your impact letter and had to read it out loud to the group. I was really afraid to read it at first and started to burst into tears. I finally read it, dad's first. Overall it wasn't bad at all, and easier than I thought. I thought it was extremeley well written and descirbed all of my past behaviors. The group was very thoughtful and kind of listening, and relating to their behaviors.

My goal is to get out of here by 3-5 weeks which everyone tells me thats impossible. I miss you already so much and many of the students here have been here for 8-12 weeks. I cant imagine being gone that long, because I really miss the family, sugar, & home.

When you get the oppurtunity please send me markers and and colored pencils, and pen, if youre allowed to. Please also respond to this telling me about how sugar and yall are. Be honest about how sugar is please. I really love ♡ miss her.

Shelter:

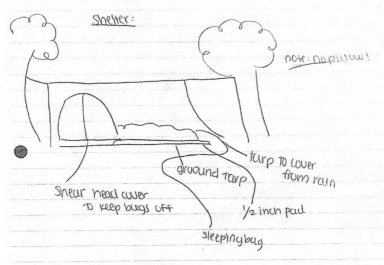

note: no pillow!

tarp to cover from rain

ground tarp

shear head cover to keep bugs off

½ inch pad

sleeping bag

please write back, love yall,

Dear Mom & Dad,

Camp is fun at times but it's really hard to stay positive when I haven't pooped in 1 week and having to sleep on 1/2 inch pad every night. Anyways the took everything away from me, accept Bear Bear. They provided me with a note pad, pen, packetwork, and a big pack of survival needs. everyone is really nice and welcoming, but I made a connection with Izzy. She's been here for two weeks, from Boulder, CO, 14 years old. Shes here from another facility and got transferred. Her parents sent her here because of drugs and alcohol. Running away too. But overall she's really, really nice & funny.

I also received your impact letter and had to read it out loud to the group. I was really afraid to read it at first and started to burst into tears. I finally read it, dad's first. Overall it wasn't bad at all, and easier than I thought. I thought it was extremely well written and described all of my past behaviors. The group was very thoughtful and kind of listening and relating to their behaviors.

My goal is to get out of here by 3-5 weeks which everyone tells me that's impossible. I miss y'all already so much and many of the students here have been here for 8-12 weeks. I can't imagine being gone that long, because I really miss the family, sugar, & home.

When you get the opportunity please send me mark-
ers and colored pencils, and pen, if you're allowed to.
Please respond to this telling me about how sugar and
y'all are. Be honest about how sugar is please. I really
love <3 miss her.

My daughter had been living in the wilderness for sev-
enty-five days when we were invited to visit her. It was time.
She was ready. On that prized summer day, we would travel
the same road we had many weeks prior, this time arriving
at the field house without our child. The therapist took the
lead as we followed her into the heavily forested Nantahala
National Park to a campsite located so deep in the woods, I
was not sure I would know my way out.

Suddenly our daughter materialized in front of my
eyes. I barely recognized her. She was thin, dirty, and covered head to toe in bug bites too numerous to count. Her
long dark hair was unkempt and haphazardly twisted into
a bun that rested on the top of her head. As I continued
to take in her appearance, tears welled up in my eyes and
I did my best to fight them off.

She greeted us in the same guarded and stoic tone she
had said goodbye with several months prior. She introduced us to her world, telling us how they hung their food
from trees at night and slept in a different location so the
animals would not bother them. She showed us the thin
mat she sat on during the day and slept on at night. She
showed us the hole they had dug in the ground that served
as a toilet. She told us how they were not allowed flash-

lights and how the counselors gathered up their shoes at night so they could not run away.

We took a short walk down a narrow dirt road to a tiny ravine where she proudly pointed out a fish she had been watching. She called our attention to a hornet's nest as she named all the trees. She described the terrifying howls of the coyotes late at night. She demonstrated the lightning drill position they were required to assume for hours at a time during a storm.

Back at camp, dark, ominous rain clouds suddenly appeared. Without warning, she sprang into action, quickly rigging a gray tarp at an angle between three trees. Once the makeshift shelter was secured, she swiftly gathered both our belongings and her backpack and delivered them to the safety of the shelter. We all sat under that tarp for several hours, while the therapist skillfully practiced her craft of healing our family.

Before the day was over, our daughter would surprise us yet again and demonstrate bow drilling, a survival skill she practiced daily. Just as she was able to transform a piece of wood through friction into a hot coal capable of starting a fire, she was also transforming before our eyes. I still did not know who she was, although there was no doubt she was courageous, brave, and strong—unlike any kid I had ever known.

As the sun began to set, she disappeared back into the wilderness and we drove off, once again putting miles between us.

When you choose the wilderness, it is not like choosing

your child's summer camp program. There are no wilderness tours. There are no cabins, no showers or toilets to check out and pass judgment on. These basics are non-existent in the wilderness. Oddly, there is no actual place at all. It truly is just what it says it is: the wilderness. It is untamed, unbroken, and serious business.

As a parent in this decision-making process, due diligence means doing the research, speaking to the program director and asking the necessary questions. Speaking to other parents who have been there and trusting the wisdom of their experience is crucial. Faith and hope are paramount because ultimately you either trust the process or you do not. For me, the decision came down to two basic choices: I could lose my daughter to the sex trade or she could be found through the power of the wilderness. I did not see any other options.

It was a long way from the comforts of home. The group, simply known as "G5," would move campsites every three to four days. Our only connection to her would be through the weekly conference calls with her therapist and the letters she wrote home. Occasionally we would receive a picture of her.

G5 would spend their days and nights carrying out the basic survival functions of life: cooking, cleaning, protecting and managing their resources. At the same time, they participated in group and individual therapy while experiencing natural therapy through the consequences of their actions or lack thereof. They endured long periods of time where they were required to sit quietly alone to reflect and journal. It was raw and it was real.

As I became familiar with the methods of wilderness therapy, I increasingly understood I had the great honor of looking behind the curtain. The lead therapist, along with the staff, was working magic in the woods. Everyone had to pull their weight for the sake of the group's intrinsic survival. There was no place to run, no place to hide. Accountability and ownership were the name of the game and eventually personal truth would rise to the surface. In the most authentic and masterful way, the perceptive therapist was paving a path for the group to find their way out of the wilderness.

Six

Transition

By the time it was all said and done, our daughter endured three months or roughly 2,160 hours apart from us in the wilderness. In my darkest nightmare, I never would have imagined ourselves in this place, so far from home, even further from the life we had known. It almost felt like it was happening to someone else.

Like an expert logistics manager, I had cleverly arranged her start date in the wilderness for June, leaving ample time for completion of the program by the end of the summer. She could return to school in the fall and no one would need to know how she spent her summer. Her issues would be addressed, resolved and fixed, and in return, I would get a new kid ready to start a new school year. In the back of my mind, I knew better. Things do not typically work that way and slowly it began to occur to me this was not a one-and-done solution.

Soon, my thoughts turned back to the present and the next series of decisions I would need to make. I could not escape the sense that her transformation had only begun. The word from camp was she had worked hard. While at the same time, she held her breath and checked the necessary boxes for the ticket home.

The integration of a strong moral code coupled with appropriate behavior had not fully taken place. How could it? She was a twelve-year-old with a child's mind who had dabbled in a sick and twisted adult world. Her psyche had been filled with distorted images that could not be wished away. For the moment, the therapist had bridled her and she conformed to the discipline of expectations. My daughter could not avoid the magnification of her life in the woods, no more than my husband and I could avoid the need to shore up her path forward. It would be negligent to bring her home before she was ready and I knew it.

In numerous letters, she made it definitively clear she was ready to come back home. In just one more month, she would turn thirteen years old and she was dreaming of her special birthday. My heart hurt for her because I already knew the truth; she would be moving on to a therapeutic boarding school and that birthday would come and go without any indulgent fanfare.

In the meantime, I was working with the educational consultant for the next placement. As promised, she had kept track of my daughter's progress in the wilderness; interfacing bi-weekly with the program's lead therapist.

When pressed directly, the therapist confirmed the uneasy feeling in the pit of my stomach and recommended against her returning home. Instead, she advocated for placement into a therapeutic boarding school.* There would be no sliding back into traditional school. I knew nothing of this proposed alternate world of boarding schools and again found myself lost in the process. I had been knocked back down to ground zero, starting anew to decipher the next step forward.

Upon reaching this new and unfamiliar crossroad, the therapist provided me with an invaluable perspective which I gratefully clung to. With great insight and wisdom, she shared the following with me: "View the situation as a jigsaw puzzle. One piece is removed and reshaped; there is no way that piece can fit back into the original puzzle. The puzzle must also change." That included our family as well as the environment in which we lived.

Upon my request, the educational consultant provided me with a list of therapeutic boarding schools based on my daughter's identified needs. This time the list was short; there were few options for middle school girls on the East Coast. I would visit both and settle on one.

Evaluating a therapeutic boarding school is a grueling process. Upon arrival to the facility, I was met by the admissions director. Without delay, I found myself launched into a concerted effort to explain why I was there and what my child needed. My head swirled with all the secret

---

* A therapeutic boarding school is an educational setting that mirrors a traditional boarding school while offering individual, group, and family therapy.

knowledge of her past. I defensively named a series of bad behaviors and poor choices she had made in order to justify my decision in seeking placement. At the same time, I was equally compelled to place her in the brightest light possible as if she were competing for a coveted position of honor. I felt like a traitor.

Next, I would meet with the Director of Clinical Services, the Dean of Academics, and the Head of the Residential Team. They were professional and patient answering my continual stream of questions. I fought to focus on each response while at the same time I battled my emotions in an effort to not become overwhelmed. Each department head would take roughly forty-five to sixty minutes to provide me with an informative overview of their program and therapeutic promises, immediately followed by a tour of the wooded property consisting of multiple acres and a tiny two-building facility.

My eyes roamed the connecting rooms, taking in the unremarkable physical details of the building. This was not a shiny, spotless well-kept facility. There was no grand hall, smartly designed living room or well-appointed bedrooms. It was somewhat worn out, with walls in need of patch work and a fresh coat of paint. The faded window curtains tilted to one side and were in need of an adjustment. In the oversized living room, a large leather sectional facing the roughhewn rock fireplace was dated and sported several stains and an occasional tear in a cushion. In the dining room, plastic blue-and-white checkered tablecloths covered the round tables, and I noticed the curious absence of glassware and knives.

The complicated lives of these girls were on display in their artwork that hung on the walls. There was no denying the pain and uncertainty in their young eyes as they fought to find their way back. I was a reluctant guest in a home that held many dark unknowns. I wondered who their parents were and whether they felt the same. Eventually, I would be left alone with two students who appeared free to answer any questions I had.

At this point, I had tons of questions. I wanted to know why they were there. Did they go willingly to the wilderness and boarding school or were they transported there? Did they like their teachers and therapists? Were they angry with their parents or at themselves? Could they see their future and, if so, what did it look like? I carefully selected my words in a bid to gain their trust and subsequent honesty. Their candor was remarkable. What stayed with me that day was a described experience of being professionally transported* to the wilderness, otherwise known by the students as having been "gooned."

A paid stranger had come into the privacy of their bedroom, unannounced in the dead of the night, abruptly waking them from a sound sleep. They were given few details other than their parents had arranged treatment for them. They were instructed to get dressed, gather a few personal items, and they would be on their way. That was it.

* *See chapter 27 for information regarding professional transport.*

It was the one event that fractured trust with their parents. It was hard for me to gauge if their relationships were mortally wounded or if they would heal with time. I looked deep into their eyes to see if I recognized my daughter.

Seven

Boarding School

She had transitioned from the wilderness to the therapeutic boarding school. It went as well as could be expected. She now had a bed to sleep in and a bathroom to share with six other students. Instead of the forest floor, she had the privilege of sitting at a table to eat. Every bit of entitlement had been swept away with a regiment of assigned daily chores. They, meaning the girls, were fully responsible for the condition in which they lived.

My daughter's life would move forward under rigorous structure. There would be no technology. Period. She was told when to wake up and when to go to bed. She was assigned a time to shower and told how long that shower could be. Hairdryers and makeup were an earned privilege. Meal times were set with little deviation and the kitchen was not open for off-hour snacks. She was responsible for her own laundry and was allowed a specific time once a week to get it done. No exceptions.

When a student eventually earned the privilege of leaving campus for dinner or an overnight visit with family, they were searched upon returning. All of their personal belongings were combed through by staff and a modified strip search was conducted. A required urine test completed the protocol for re-entry to the campus. It was necessary for the safety of the community. Guilty or not, there were no exceptions.

By this point, she was fully aware of what loss of freedom meant. She would live day and night with roughly twenty-five students. They would eat together, study together, and do therapy together. If there was a problem, and there were plenty of problems, they would work it out face-to-face together.

After thirty days, she would earn the privilege of a phone call home. In the boarding school's common living room, discreetly located off to one side, were six connected doorless stalls, each outfitted with a telephone and a backless stool. A staff member was assigned to place and monitor the call on the students' behalf. Upon confirming who they were speaking to, the staff member would pass the phone to the student. It felt like a call from prison. The same day of the week, at the same time and for the same fifteen minutes, with the same talking points. It was clear she hated the school, and everyone else was crazy and she obviously did not belong there. She would alternate between anger and tears as she begged to come home. They were tough calls and I dreaded them.

Two months in, we would go to our first mandatory parent seminar. I was unprepared for what came next. On the first day of the seminar, the parents were asked to gather in a plain conference room. After small talk and coffee, the seminar leaders introduced themselves and then asked us each to stand and introduce ourselves. They encouraged us to share with the group who our daughter was, how long she had been part of the community, and a little bit about her. As I started to speak, I was overwhelmed by the involuntary rush of my emotions. For the first time, I was telling the story of my daughter out loud, in front of strangers no less, with nowhere to hide. There were thirty people or so in that room, and with each unguarded personal account, the energy became heavier. These people laid themselves and their pain wide open. Their raw and exposed narratives ranged from total despair and heartbreak to glimpses of hope for the future. Silent tears slid down my face as I listened to the details of their tormented stories. I had never witnessed another human's anguish in such a vulnerable and personal way.

I remained transfixed in my chair as faceless strangers continued to emerge and transform into desperate devoted parents. The fear of judgment lifted, as I realized we all were fighting a battle to save our daughters. This was new to me and I did my best to not become emotionally unraveled.

In that moment, my circumstances felt small where my daughter was concerned. I had been proactive and managed to sidestep the deeper, more complex issues of alcohol, drugs, and physical contact with sexual predators. Some of the parents had not been so fortunate. I was grateful I had not ignored the unsettled feeling I had early on. I was grateful to no longer feel alone.

Later, we would split off into smaller groups that included our daughters. The new assignment was family sculpting. Family sculpting is a therapeutic technique in which the therapist asks one of the family members, in this case the daughter in treatment, to arrange their families in the way they currently perceive them to be. The first family took the center of the room. The daughter arranged her parents on opposite sides of the room with their backs to each other. She told her mom to pretend to be on the phone and her father to passively sit in front of a make-believe television. She arranged her little brother off to one side playing on a computer. She herself sat down in the opposite corner of the room with her knees pulled up to her chest where she proceeded to anxiously rock back and forth. After several silent minutes, the therapist then directed her to rearrange her family the way she would like to see them. She pulled her parents together, had them place their arms around each other, and asked them to smile and look into each other's eyes. She then directed her brother away from his imaginary computer and placed him next to the parents where she also quietly stood. This was her ideal family. It was a powerful visual of a child's basic desire.

Eight

A Bit of Levity

One of the bigger challenges came from the outside. The dreaded onslaught of questions from well-intended family members, inquisitive friends, and even strangers that were not in the know. Basically, their curiosity was innocent but problematic. Shame would creep in as I tried to handle the finer points of my double life. I was an all-or-nothing sort of girl. It was not easy to know what to say when your mind is on fire and you do not have a poker face. When pressed on my daughter's whereabouts, I would sometimes reveal too much and other times I would say nothing at all. Either way, I sought to protect my daughter while still presenting her in a positive light. With time, I learned how to skillfully manage the questions and even have a little fun with it.

One particular incident comes to mind when my more roguish side emerged. Clearly, I could not help myself.

A stranger struck up a conversation and proceeded to openly brag about her daughter's acceptance into a very prestigious boarding school in Australia. According to her, the entrance standards were very rigorous; therefore, few were admitted. Her daughter, an academic prodigy, was destined to be important in the field of medicine. In a polite turn, she asked me about my daughter. I took a moment and then with total pleasure said the following: "Well, my daughter is also in a boarding school, actually located in North Carolina. Her school is so exclusive that hardly anyone is admitted. You cannot believe the requirements to get in. The things she had to do were endless and fairly unbelievable. The entire process took several years of consistent effort. In addition, a student must demonstrate advanced knowledge in technology and even then, it is difficult to gain entrance. She is going places!" I cannot deny the level of satisfaction I derived from that conversation.

If I looked hard enough, there were other places in which to find humor. My daughter left for the wilderness with only the clothes on her back. Everything in her world as she knew it was left behind, including all things having to do with technology. There would be no cell phone, no iPad or laptop, and not even an iPod. In my daughter's universe, this translated into zero outside communication and no electronic entertainment of any sort, including games, movies, and music.

It would be many months later when she would earn back the privilege of one simple iPod and the freedom to once again enjoy music. When that day came, I must admit, I recognized a rare opportunity to dump the music I hated and found so highly offensive. Here laid the perfect circumstance to redirect her. Before mailing her iPod, I scrubbed it clean and then proceeded to take control by downloading all of my music which included the best of the 60s, 70s, and 80s. Keeping her in mind, I added a handful of her favorite current hits, but only the ones I also liked. There was a nod to country music, featuring Waylon Jennings, Willie Nelson, and Johnny Cash, who turned out to be her favorite outlaw. Finally, I rounded it out with a bit of the classic standards such as Frank Sinatra and Louis Armstrong. Her appreciation of different genres grew expeditiously, and suddenly we had some wonderful music in common. I was amused and delighted, while at the same time aware of the small connection created between the two of us. I considered this a tiny victory.

Nine

The Partnership

I suspect my husband is like a lot of men. If there is a problem, he immediately seeks a solution and expects a result. That is how it usually works in his life.

But this was different.

The journey of a wounded child does not have a definitive end. Time becomes suspended and has little meaning in the therapeutic world. It does not "get fixed." Rather, it gets integrated and healed in such a way that one forgives oneself and is able to live with it.

It is an ongoing, arduous process. Most notably it becomes part of the fabric of who that child eventually becomes. That is also true for those who take the journey with her.

It was fortunate my husband did not see the evidence of our child's misdeeds. It was something a father should never witness where his daughter is concerned. This was his baby girl and he chose to push away the unthinkable and only see her in the best light possible.

Seeing the best in people was my husband's natural inclination despite a particularly stinging and painful incident that occurred prior to her treatment. He regrettably became the direct recipient of one of her more hateful behaviors. One evening upon his return from work, he entered the house through our back door and headed enthusiastically toward our young daughter who sat on a barstool at the kitchen island. He grabbed her into a massive bear hug, said hello and planted a big kiss on her head. Revolted, she jerked away and in a sinister voice filled with loathing said, "Don't hug me, you are not my father. Get away from me. I hate you." Dumbstruck, he retreated.

I stood there in shocked disbelief of what I had just witnessed. Upset and alarmed, I immediately ran multiple scenarios through my head. My mind flooded with the worst of possibilities. There were plenty of teenagers running around our house, and I wondered if someone had taken advantage of her. Had she been sexually abused? Had someone done something to her? I delicately questioned her around this possibility. I thoroughly and extensively questioned my older children concerning their behavior as well as their friends. I painfully questioned my husband. With a high degree of certainly, I ruled out sexual abuse, yet I knew something was amiss. It would be two years later, while she was in treatment, that I would finally make the connection of what happened that day.

My daughter had been repeatedly exposed much earlier and much longer to internet pornography than I had known. This nightmare had begun when she was barely ten years old.

Often my husband and I did not agree on how to proceed. There was a lot of push and pull; both of us were desperately passionate about our position. Some days we could barely discuss the situation, and our conversations would end on a heated note; this was especially true during her time in boarding school. More than once, he found himself at the point of vehemently insisting we bring her home and put an end to what felt like absurdity. The more she acted out, the less it looked like progress was being made and the closer she came to a ticket home. It was in these contentious moments when I would ask God to reveal a direction to me. I knew bringing her home before she was ready would be a disastrous misstep. On multiple occasions and in the precise moment of need, I was always granted enough grace and clarity to make a sound decision, enabling me to gain confidence in the path forward.

Her behavior was a paradox. As each defiant explosive action shot to the surface, she became further exposed and enraged. As a result, the therapist was given something more substantial to work with. In the oddest of ways, it was a gift—the one I had been waiting for. No doubt we were standing on a slippery slope, and the troubled behavior that landed her in this position was the bedrock that would provide the foothold for healing. Ultimately, it allowed me to form a compelling case for continuing treatment for our daughter. The end result was my husband yielding to my recommendation. This became a rinse-and-repeat cycle.

I was on the front lines and remained there for the duration of the struggle. He hated to see her suffer and would sometimes exit into the shadows. It was hard on him. He would escape deep into the demands of work. Together we mourned the loss of her teenage years. Gone was the first dance, the first day of high school, homecoming, a first kiss, and turning sweet sixteen. We watched as each of these rites of passage somberly slipped away and eventually vanished with the passing of time. It was a tough pill to swallow.

In the beginning, our daughter's conspicuous absence put a strain on my mental state. My mind and energy were centered around her day and night with little room for anyone else. I felt if I diverted my attention away from her, I would somehow be delinquent in my efforts and she would be lost to me forever. Gradually, I determined this was not so. For the first time in years, I had unexpected freedom that left me feeling guilty and in a pensive mood. Step by step I learned to manage my new set of responsibilities while also starting to live life again. I began to enjoy my newfound independence. My husband and I were able to rediscover our relationship. A sense of spontaneity returned to our daily lives and it felt good.

At the same time, our commitment to our daughter's treatment put pressure on the family resources: money, time and energy. We re-ordered our lives to meet her needs. As a result, the decision was made to significantly downsize our home and simplify our lives. We temporarily moved into an apartment until we could determine our next move. Interestingly, these unforeseen circumstances were liberating and brought us together at a very necessary time. It was energizing. We felt renewed as we blazed a new path together. We trusted each other on a different level and played to the other person's strengths. My husband's answer was to work harder. He did work harder, and it gave him great comfort to be able to provide. My answer was to stay present and on the path toward restoring our daughter to wholeness.

Ten

Homeward Bound

Our daughter had been away from home for a little over three years. During that time, she had completed wilderness, middle school, and was now in her second year of high school. She had lived apart from us for so long, I could hardly remember what it was like to have her home. I was not sure if she would ever live with us again, nor was I sure she would want to. I had built a new life around her absence that became my functioning norm. She had also adapted, living life among strangers who would in the end become a different type of family.

At times, I had to revisit the circumstances that lead us to this place to begin with. My thoughts would occasionally blur between the past and present, intermixing the many reasons that were the driving force behind my initial actions. It became more difficult to separate the original intent and current need. As she evolved, so did the questions surrounding what the future held. The new question became: Who was I accommodating and what was I accomplishing; was it still about her?

Yes, at the age of twelve, I instantly shut down her world, removed her from society, and tucked her away in a closed environment void of technology. I was fully aware she would be completely cut off from social media and the outside world, and at times that would include me. I knew I had set her up where her behaviors would be exposed and she would be held accountable for her actions, at times suffering harsh consequences as a result. No, I did not realize the degree of control I was giving up, nor did I understand what relinquishing power over my child would feel like. Nonetheless, this was precisely what was required of me. I could not interfere if I wanted her to succeed in the program. The school would determine the dates, times, and length of our phone calls. The school would determine if she was in good standing to leave campus for a visit. Phone calls and outings were earned privileges and would hold little value if I intervened, undermining the process. Intellectually I understood, but emotionally, I did not know how agonizing this could be.

All the while, in the back of my mind, I wondered when it would be enough. Where was the magic finish line that would guarantee her success? When was it time for her to come home and how would I know? Life at a therapeutic boarding school had provided her with lessons of societal norms and mores as well as occasional lessons of the law. The constant structure kept her safe and accountable. I could sleep at night knowing a set of eyes were on her twenty-four hours a day, seven days a week. There was comfort in that arrangement.

Every now and then, someone at the boarding school would get out of hand and the sheriff was called. On more than one occasion, a student would find herself arrested and handcuffed for assault or destruction of property and taken to the local jail. It was Real-Life Consequences 101 and there was no downplaying bad behavior.

Within the boarding school walls, a mini gang of six girls had formed. One day the group rebelled during a community meeting. This was not the first time. As their disruptive and defiant behavior began to escalate, the tension in the room increased expeditiously, creating a direct conflict between themselves and the other girls. The brash gang refused to stand down and ramped things up with explicitly rough language. Those not interested in the riotous uprising were quickly escorted into a classroom where the doors were locked. In turn, the rest of the school went on lockdown. The band of six continued to spiral out of control as they roamed the campus at will and began to throw furniture. Their war cries echoed throughout the hallways as they terrorized the sequestered students by banging on the classroom windows with their bare hands until the glass shattered. The staff immediately set in action the protocol to manage and contain the rapidly growing situation until reinforcements in the form of the county sheriff could arrive. The ramifications of the gang's unruly and violent behavior were soon to become their legal reality as law enforcement took control. They would be held culpable.

The incident left an indelible impression on my daughter. She also lived with her own inner truth; the insight of what it feels like to rage inside uncontrollably, spewing animosity toward anyone who was unfortunate enough to cross her path. She now knew what it was like to experience someone else's direct unsparing wrath. It was unnerving and terrifying. The roles had been reversed, completing a full circle lesson. I was awestruck by the power of such a moment.

Ironically, I had managed to place her in an isolation booth away from the troubled world of technology, but not the unpredictable world of angry young teenagers. The reality was that on occasion she would be exposed to criminal behavior, albeit within a controlled environment. Be that as it may, my daughter was experiencing what it felt like to sacrifice her freedom and family, a chilling preview to a life lived out of control.

In the outside world, all the nefarious forces I had fought against would be back in play, and I was petrified I would not be ready. I was horror-struck at the thought of losing control of her again.

As weeks turned into months and months turned into years, a growing awareness of our daughter's absence in our family's living history became more apparent. It was not just the holidays and special occasions slipping quietly by, it was the subtle things that happen in a family. The private sometimes tasteless jokes, the embarrassing blush-worthy moments, and the deep disappointments that bond a family together in solidarity. They were gone; lost to her forever.

She was now sixteen years old and there would only be a couple more years before she was no longer under our legal custody. It was time for her to come home.

Her years away from us made her unique and extraordinary. I would never fully understand what it was like to be her, how could I? I would never know what it felt like to involuntarily leave home, sleep on the forest floor night after night, and not know when it would end. I would never understand what it was like to return to school after a weekend away and be searched like a common criminal; nor what it feels like to be questioned by the police regarding the actions of a roommate.

What I did understand is that it made her different. Remarkably, she was not bitter and she valued her family fiercely. She was independent, responsible, and disciplined. She was no longer entitled and greatly appreciated the smallest of gestures. She was uncommonly resourceful and quietly observant. She was aware. She was a survivor.

I needed to remind myself she was not the same little girl I had taken to the wilderness all those many months ago. Upon her return, there would be no such thing as life returning to normal. In fact, the old normal would not only be impossible to recreate, but would be doomed to failure. Much like the past three-and-a-half years, I did not know what the path forward looked like, but I knew we would forge it together.

January 30, 2020

Dear Daughter,

I have been struggling with what words of wisdom I can impart to you . . . but I do not have any.

All I have is the truth as I know it. There are certain universal laws that don't ever change no matter what you are going through or how old you are.

Consider the following:

You will never be able to fully hide from yourself. *You may be able to trick or out-smart me or others around you, maybe even yourself at times. But the truth is, you and your creator will always know.*

How you choose to live your life comes down to a series of decisions. *There is not one incident or choice that got you to where you currently are or will get you to where you are going.*

You can only control yourself. *You can't change another person, but you can change what you do and, in doing so, change the reaction/outcome you get.*

What you put out is what you get back.

No effort in = no reward out. If you do the work, the reward will be beyond anything you could imagine.

You have the power of choice. *People are not doing "things" to you. You decide the how and why of your actions.*

So, what does this have to do with you? After nearly four years of a therapeutic environment, you have checked a lot of boxes and now it's time to make some decisions. You are standing at the fork in the road and your direction is purely up to you. The truth is, I can't decide for you . . . I can and will continue to support and direct you, mainly because I love you and believe in your ability to be an outstanding individual. I believe you have strength and courage that you don't even know you have. I believe this journey has great purpose because I believe in God, and He is greater than me.

You have greatly affected my life in ways you will never understand. I am however grateful, as it has made me the mother I am. Know that I don't regret that you are my child.

Love,

Mom

Eleven

Home

The house she came back to was not the home she had left. We had moved two years earlier into a much smaller townhouse in a different part of the city. Gone was the yard, the pool, and the only neighborhood she had ever lived in.

As I packed up our lives, I was careful not to erase hers. There were clothes she had outgrown and toys she would no longer play with. In many ways, she had shed her childhood innocence, yet she was at times still childlike. It was difficult to know which possessions held meaning for her. As I sorted through her belongings, I was overwhelmed by memories that left me transfixed in the past. I wanted to rid her of the things that caused pain and anchored her to a previous life; yet they were the authentic pieces responsible for creating her future. It was important I not betray her.

I put away the framed photographs that did not represent our family as a whole. Something told me she would notice and look about to see if she found herself in the photos displayed in our home. It was a test of belonging. She needed to know the door had not closed behind her and there was still a seat at the table.

At last, she was home. I felt a tremendous sense of loss over the past several years she lived apart from us. When she would let me, I blissfully tucked her into bed, an action resulting in an unexpected deluge of emotions on my part. Deep regret swept over me as I realized all the nights I had not been able to simply kiss my daughter goodnight and tell her I loved her before she drifted off to sleep. The very thought broke my heart; I can only imagine what it did to a young girl who still needed her mother.

When given the chance, I would do simple things for her. Ridiculously simple, from turning down her bed at night to leaving fresh flowers on the corner of her desk. I was desperate to make up for the lost years. I needed to nurture her in order to heal myself.

Her first days and weeks at home, she was cautious around me, like a polite house guest who was careful to not give a reason to be dismissed. She made her bed and tidied her room without being prompted. She hung around after dinner and helped clean the kitchen. She sought permission without assumptions. To her credit, her instincts were razor sharp; she knew I held no empty threats and would not tolerate any behaviors of the past.

I would stare at her as if I was seeing her for the first

time. I studied her features and found myself in her face. She was no longer a child, but a young adult whose eyes were filled with knowing. Her physical presence was strong and confident. She was unassuming yet difficult to read. At the same time, she was authentically powerful. And on the rare occasion she chose to offer it, her smile could light up a room.

Nonetheless, I remained consumed with creating a no-fail zone, and for the next five months did not leave her side for any extended period of time. The smallest of distractions diverting my attention away from her felt like an inherent threat fueled by the worst of my imagination. As a result, she continued to live life with limited technology and I had yet to provide her with a smartphone. I was nervous and jumpy, while she was patient and tolerant of my efforts to protect her. She had been living tech-free for close to four years—a lifetime for a teenager.

Her seventeenth birthday was fast approaching, and the one gift she wanted more than anything else in the world was the one I did not want to give her: a smartphone. What appeared to otherwise be a typical teenage request left me a nervous wreck and seriously conflicted. I deeply valued the person she had become. She had developed an amazing memory and ability to recall information. Her handwriting was old school and beautiful. She could endure long meaningful conversations and enjoy the company of adults. I loved that about her! The last thing I wanted was a smartphone and social media to gobble it all up and once again take my daughter away from me. I felt like I was standing on the edge of the final frontier, with no option but to move forward. It was time to trust her.

The passage of time had unnaturally evaporated as I witnessed my little girl transform into a young woman who would soon meet the world on her own adult terms. There remained a precious and small window of opportunity to ensure her safety in a world of technology, one which would surely be part of her future.

Twelve

The After Story

It took close to nine months for her to decompress and begin to create a new normal. At the same time, we were in the middle of the Covid-19 pandemic of 2020. In the strangest of ways, the restrictions imposed on our lives provided me the time and slow pace I desired to re-establish our life together. We occupied the same space all day, every day for weeks on end. She was not perfect, but she was willing, and as a result we always found our footing.

The first order of business was enrolling her in high school. I focused on identifying a small controlled environment with accountability and high expectations. That meant private schools. Ironically, I quickly discovered several Christian private schools I had considered were not interested in a student who had been in therapeutic boarding school. These types of students made admission directors nervous. Their experience was they often revert back to troubled behavior and find it difficult to fit in socially and academically. My older children had attended private schools and I was not naive regarding the admissions process, but I did not anticipate this reaction, and it left me anxious and discouraged, not to mention angry.

Initial contact with the private schools had been made by an educational consultant on my behalf. Ironically, one of the schools under consideration my daughter had attended from kindergarten through third grade before transferring to a public school. The other school on the short list was one my older children had attended and graduated from. Our family had been part of the church community from the day our children were baptized. We had financially supported both institutions for years through our yearly tuition, annual giving, and capital campaign donations, not to mention our time and energy. How could it be that they were unwilling to entertain a student application and interview? Where were the Christian values? Where was the forgiveness and grace for a child who had made mistakes? My daughter and I had been swiftly dismissed and thoughtlessly abandoned in our time of need and it hurt.

My options were quickly diminishing, and I felt the sting of being ostracized. I genuinely believed they would be fortunate to receive my daughter. She had done more interpersonal work than most forty-year-old people have or ever will. Her formative years were spent in a high-accountability environment without social media. At the same time, she accepted and understood full ownership of all personal decisions. In addition, she alone was held responsible for the state of her academics. She had fought her way back and I believed she had earned a chance. Why could they not see this?

I remained resolute and continued to aggressively advocate for my daughter, making several impassioned phone calls on her behalf until she received an interview. From that moment forward, she stood on her own, securing her acceptance into the school.

Then, there were my private concerns. Would she share too much of her boarding school experience? Would she reveal too many details of why she had been away in the first place? Would she be too trusting of other kids with her secrets? Conversely, I worried she would be out of sync with her peers and find it difficult to relate. Therapeutic boarding school had advanced her beyond her years, leaving her averse to teenage game playing and manipulation. Only time would tell.

Again, the Covid-19 pandemic proved to be a contentious ally. The first month of school was held virtually, allowing her time to observe her new peers from afar. By the time students were allowed on campus, she was more than eager to meet her new classmates in person. Not surprisingly, she was immediately barraged with questions regarding social media. Did she have a Facebook page and Instagram? What social media did she have? Her plain-spoken and direct answer was "No, I do not." Naturally, the follow-up question was: Why not? She appeared indifferent, offering little explanation when she replied,

"Because I'm not interested."

Very quickly she learned the absence of a social platform made her unique and, in some ways, came with additional benefits. Occasionally at school, situations requiring disciplinarian action arose and were brought to the attention of the administration. The complaints almost always involved social media in one form or another. My daughter was happy to opt out of any accusations or scrutiny regarding her use of social media. I silently breathed a sigh of relief, thankful she recognized and valued her unusual position.

The balancing act of her independence with the rules of home was somewhat tedious in the beginning; resembling a controlled tug-of-war. She would often remind me she had lived without me for quite some time and did not need my constant supervision. At the same time, she would appear helpless when it came to performing the simplest of tasks. I found her independence to be wonderfully refreshing and simultaneously nerve-racking. Consequently, these mixed messages would leave me frustrated and resentful; however, I still was not willing to forgo my parental duties in an effort to appease my teenage daughter.

Without question, my parenting style needed frequent realignment in order to match my daughter's evolving personality. The young, unruly child I took to the woods had disappeared and remained forever banished to the past. In her place emerged a respectful young lady who knew how to effectively advocate for herself. Our relationship had been undoubtedly altered with a new challenge of determining what household rules needed to be permanently left behind and those that needed to be carefully preserved. This was the tricky part.

All the while, I too struggled with my revoked freedom and the adjustment of having her home once again. I was solidly tethered to her daily needs while my personal life and plans were restricted, and in some cases put on hold. I sought to find the equilibrium that would satisfy us both.

I eventually began to relax and find my stride. A visit to the doctor's office left both of us cracking up. As part of her wellness checkup, the doctor suggested when she became too stressed out and overwhelmed, she should find a space in which she could stomp her feet and scream as long and loud as she wanted. Bursting into laughter, I looked at the doctor and said with considerable amusement, "We just paid a fortune for boarding school and therapy to get her *not* to do that very thing!"

Was every decision made along the way the correct one? No, but I believe we made more right decisions than wrong ones. Do we know how her time in the wilderness and therapeutic boarding schools will forever manifest itself in her life? Of course not. Her evolution is an ongoing process. Were the years she spent apart from our family worth the pain and sacrifices? Yes, I believe it was. Gone is the rage, anger, and intolerance of others around her and in its place is her desire to have a relationship with her family.

I continue to receive validation in the smallest of ways. In her actions, offhanded comments, and unguarded moments. To my astonishment, she entertains the idea of being a mentor to others in the wilderness. She craves structure and does her best to build it around her. In addition, she keeps a watchful eye on her future, doing her best to safeguard the investment she has made in herself.

At the same time, she bristles at any conversation regarding the past. It is behind her and she does not wish to resurrect it. I do my best to respect that, but to my way of thinking, it is a strong testimony of an individual who demonstrated an ability to endure and rise to the occasion. I hope one day she will see this as an accomplishment and not a place to dwell in shame.

Do I have concerns and fears regarding her future choices? Yes, it is always in the back of my mind. However, I expect that will begin to fade with time until eventually they are just a thing in the past. I have no regrets; I know I did not fall short. I stayed with her every step of the way and will continue to do so.

Thirteen

How Did I Do It?

At first, I was not really sure how I did it. Then I realized it was not just one thing, it was a series of events that fostered insight and a growing awareness of a child who was increasingly becoming entangled in adversity. As a result, the following observations are what ultimately contributed to paving a path for our daughter to find her way back.

Do not ignore the behavior. The challenges with my daughter came early; at three years old she was energetic and spirited, with a mind of her own. She was cute with a dimpled cheek, curly hair, and a big personality, capable of commanding a room and upending the collective mood in a split second. With each disruptive incident, she became more intensely out of control and I vowed to tighten the disciplinary screws on her unruly behavior. I had a tiger by the tail and it was not long before I was being stretched beyond my parental abilities. Each day brought a newly revised plan of strategic child discipline until I had exhausted my repertoire of knowledge. Despite all of my efforts, the more I tried, the more she dug in until she effectively blocked me out of her life. By age ten, she had succeeded in forging an impermeable barrier around herself; leaving me on the outside with seemingly nowhere to go.

Do not run or look away. The next several years, we would continue to struggle, experiencing alternating bouts of optimism and pessimism as I tried to crack her behavioral code. She was at her best when we were in sync with no opposing forces and at her worst when direction abruptly changed, rendering plans unpredictable. I tapped all possibilities from medicinal management to therapeutic interventions, even locating a group for young girls that focused on life skills. Unfortunately, even that ended badly.

Since she did not care for group therapy, maybe she would prefer individual therapy. As it turned out, she did not care for either, as evidenced the day she threw a shoe at the therapist. At the same time, I intentionally selected books with positive messages and strategically placed them around the house, hoping they would resonate with her. Disappointingly, the books remained untouched, retaining their wisdom while collecting dust. I ventured to go further; maybe a change of schools along with a new group of kids would be a solution. It proved to be only a temporary fix, as it took a bit more time to run her predictable cycle of making friendships and subsequently sabotaging them.

I did everything I knew to do, until I did not know of anything more. Every carefully planned intervention failed and every thoughtful word collapsed the day the dreadful truth was exposed. That fateful moment I checked her smartphone, accidentally coming across private screenshots not intended for my eyes, was the instant everything changed. The captured screen began to tell the story of my daughter; a foreboding narrative that could not be taken back. It was beyond unbearable to read the distasteful texts and even worse to view the shocking pictures. I had unknowingly come upon the wreckage of an active crime scene, but I did not look away. Now I knew without a doubt, I was the prison watch guard and not the trusted confidant I hoped to be. My daughter was barely twelve years old.

Trust your intuition. It was impossible to shake the anxious feeling that stayed with me day and night, inconspicuously draining me until I was on edge and unsettled. It was an incessant reminder to give credence to the tiny voice inside my head that continued to sound the alarm bells. I did not fully understand the scope of the situation and struggled to wrap my mind around things I could not conceive of as I worked to fill in the missing pieces. There was no denying something was terribly wrong and I would need to be patient as validation would come in time. Meanwhile, I moved through what felt like a thick fog bank, leaving me surrounded in complete darkness with little definition and giving no indication of what was to come. At the same time, I knew. I knew it would be up to me to handle what came next. I knew I would be the bridge between her past and her future. It would be my commitment that would make the difference between her remaining lost or being found. I would need to trust God and the voice inside my head to know the way forward. I believed a pathway would be revealed as long as I remained open to it and willing to accept it. That moment of blind faith was the first of many to come.

Do not interfere with the process. This was especially difficult when it came to the boarding schools. It was part of my parent DNA to stay in control. I had vowed to be her protector the day she was born, helping her avert disaster regarding things she had yet to understand. It was my duty to teach spiritual values and provide moral guidance regardless of any outside forces. In my mind, this is what responsible parents did, and I would be held ultimately accountable for my actions or lack thereof.

This did not automatically change the day she entered therapeutic boarding school. In a reversal of roles, the school now experienced my daughter's daily combative behavior and I became the secondary onlooker. The program would drive the treatment plan, at times purposely placing her in uncomfortable and challenging situations in which she would be held accountable for her behavior; essentially providing an opportunity for her to fail in order to learn. It was difficult to watch. Simultaneously, the school consistently enforced tough consequences for violating the rules of the community. It was distressing to stand on the sidelines and let them do their jobs. I found myself wanting in-depth details in order to judge the situation. I was not always privileged to the information I wanted and I did not like it. Over time, I would come to appreciate that life in a therapeutic boarding school was often convoluted and did not easily lend itself to micro communication with worried parents. Basically, it boiled down to picking when and where I would interject myself.

Moreover, I understood the interaction between the therapist and my daughter was crucial. More importantly to note, the relationship between therapist and client is privileged and confidential, legally protected by law. I paid the bill, but in this case, I was not the client. That meant I would never be fully entitled to the specifics regarding their conversations unless my daughter chose to disclose them to me. It was not only frustrating but scary to be intermittently blocked from the details of her progress, but I would need to accept it and stay out of the way if there was to be any hope of healing. It was that simple.

Become part of the solution. I learned to ask a very important question: *What can I do to help my daughter move forward?* I meant it with every ounce of my being and would do anything for this child. My commitment was genuine and proved to be a difference maker as I slowly built a powerful alliance with the school. I did not always get it right, but I remained a willing and active participant in the process, regardless of my personal feelings or opinions.

Without fail, I attended the mandatory parent seminars every quarter despite the additional financial expense and inconvenient scheduling. I participated weekly in emotional family therapy sessions regardless of how unpleasant they sometimes became. I wrote my daughter long letters and accepted her weekly phone calls, when at times I admittedly did not feel like it.

When given the opportunity, I asked questions and sought solutions. Sometimes I did not like the feedback I received concerning my parenting style and would become sensitive and defensive. I worked to keep the recommendations presented by the therapist and school staff in perspective, while at the same time bearing in mind neither were infallible. I had the right to override the school or withdraw my daughter at any given time. I was still the parent.

I considered ways to benefit the community. I searched for a way to connect with my daughter and the girls she was living her life with. With this in mind, I approached the director and asked to share my passion and expertise in floral design with the school community. To my delight, she welcomed my idea with an enthusiastic yes.

The floral class was scheduled the day before the parent seminar. I arrived toting large buckets filled with hundreds and hundreds of fresh, colorful flowers. It was not long before the dining hall resembled a spring garden bursting with beautiful possibilities. As several curious and excited girls peeked around the corner, I was deeply moved to see the light of pure happiness in their eyes. It was everything that was good and innocent and perfect all at once. It was sweet and unguarded. It was a rarified moment in time and the reward for my efforts was unexpected and greater than I could have imagined.

As I slowly began to teach the girls floral craft with meticulously planned step-by-step instructions, some exuberantly charged ahead abandoning my guided directions, prompting me to say, "Flowers are art, and art is beauty. There is no right or wrong here, only a unique creation as the artist sees it. You are the artist." Just like the girls, the arrangements were beautiful yet different. Some were formal and tamed while others were free and wild.

What are you supposed to be learning? The perspective this question brought was invaluable; not to mention life-changing. When I learned to re-frame what was happening in my family, and ask myself "What am I supposed to be learning?" events took on a different meaning. We were anything but unfortunate victims. The events of my daughter's life created a ripple effect that touched many people and points along the way. The possibilities for personal growth were unexpected gateways into something more significant. On one hand, what was a very painful sequence of events, morphed into an undeniable gift of a lifetime.

PART TWO

The Research

Introduction

*II*It has become appallingly obvious that our technology has exceeded our humanity."

This quote was not said in direct reference to today's technology and social media. Rather, the origins of this quote are debatable. Albert Einstein was thought to have said something to this effect in 1946 regarding the nuclear age.

Just as the consequences of the development of the atomic bomb has affected and altered our world, so has the use and development of technology as we know it today. As a society, we have yet to fully understand the ramifications of the internet and social media. I would argue however, we are sadly beginning to see much of the by-product. The emerging outcome in my opinion has been detrimental to our society and particularly to our youth. Notably a different type of destruction of human life.

Fourteen

Social Media and
Internet Statistics

Where do you start when trying to make an impact on a teenager regarding technology? My first impulse was to look at the statistics surrounding technology and social media and present the facts. Observable behavior would suggest our society has been saturated by an ongoing need and, more importantly, desire for devices with technological capabilities. To what degree would this prove to be true?

My mission was personal, and I wondered if I had allowed the monsters in the dark to take over. Was it really as serious as I imagined? Did it really matter? After all, practically everyone I know is on Facebook or Instagram. Was it a young person's pastime or any person's pastime?

Everywhere I looked I found social media—in every crevice of our society. Families in restaurants, smartphones in hand, all looking down to check on Yelp what other people ordered. Oftentimes quickly followed by carefully crafted pictures of their menu selection to post on Instagram. More concerning is the abundance of people texting and driving, to the point we now have laws addressing this behavior. Finally, I could not help but notice the influencers, imagined and otherwise, posing everywhere and anywhere for a real-time social media post.

Now, more recently and unexpectedly, technology has become the lifeline holding our world together as the Coronavirus weaves itself into our daily lives. With few options available, school children take instruction online, parents work online, businesses run online. We have turned to virtual workouts, Zoom happy hours, and Face-Time family gatherings. Strangely, we have never been more intricately connected yet physically isolated.

It is imperative to consider the presented statistics with the events of the Coronavirus pandemic in mind. It is yet to be determined how people will choose to react to the life-altering events of 2020. The time has never been more critical for parents to be vigilant in a society that has been driven online.

Details and Data

"Privacy is dead, and social media holds the smoking gun."[1] —*Pete Cashmore, founder of the blog Mashable*

Social Media Platforms and Use (adult habits ages 18–29)

Seven out of every ten Americans (or 69% of the population) use social media to connect with one another.

- 88% of those are between the ages of 18–29.
- 74% use Facebook on a daily basis.
- 63% use Snapchat on a daily basis.
- 60% use Instagram on a daily basis.
- 46% use Twitter on a daily basis.
- 45% use YouTube on a daily basis.

2019 YouTube Statistics

- We watch over 1 billion hours of video each day.
- 400 hours of video are uploaded every minute.
- One billion video views (on average) per day.

2019 Instagram Statistics

- As of 2018, there are more than 1 billion users on Instagram.
- There are 500 million daily active users.

2019 Snapchat Statistics

- 60% of Snapchat users are under the age of 25.
- 78% of all Americans ages 18–24 use Snapchat.
- 47% of US teens think Snapchat is better than Facebook.

2019 Facebook Statistics

- Facebook is where people spend most of their social media time.
- FB reaches approximately 97% of people between ages 18–34.[2]

2021 TikTok Statistics

- Over 689 million active users worldwide.[3]
- 63% of users are 10–29 years old.[4]
- Recent report: children 4–15 years old used TikTok during the peak of the United States quarantine (March 15–April 2020) for an average of 86 minutes a day.[5]

Globally, there were 3.196 billion social media users in 2018.[6]

Communication

Number of times a smartphone is checked in a typical hour:

- 27% check 5–9 times/hour.
- 25% check 10–14 times/hour.
- 24% check 30 or more times/hour.
- 14% check 20–24 times/hour.
- 8% check 15–19 times/hour.
- 2% check 25–29 time/hour.[7]

Social Media Platforms and Use (teen habits, ages 13–17)

- 90% of American teens (who own cell phones) text.
- Girls aged 13–17 typically send and receive 40 texts/day.
- 50% use video chat services (such as Zoom and FaceTime).
- 85% use YouTube.
- 72% use Instagram.
- 69% use Snapchat.
- 51% use Facebook (down from 71% in 2015).
- 32% use Twitter.[8]

Smartphone Statistics Worldwide

- There are 3.5 billion users around the world. (The population of the world is 7.6 billion.) Translation: 1 in 3 people own a cell phone.
- There were 204 billion app downloads in 2019 (the majority being games).
- Mobile apps are projected to generate 201 billion US dollars in revenue by 2021.

Smartphone Usage Statistics

- 20% of millennials open an app at least 50 times a day.
- 71% of teenagers watch an average of over 3

hours of video online daily.

- 78% of teenagers now have access to a mobile device.
- 53% of teenagers now value social media followers equal to social currency.
- 50% of smartphone owners now check mobile devices first thing in the morning.[9]
- As of January 2021, 5.22 billion people (66.6% of the global population) use a mobile device.
- 40% of American adults report giving their child a cell phone by the age of 10.
- 94% of participants in a Facebook study held their smartphones while watching television.
- 75% of Americans admit to bringing their mobile phone into the bathroom.
- Over 1 billion hours of video content are viewed on YouTube every day.[10]

How Much Money Does the Mobile Ecosystem Generate?

- The global mobile ecosystem generated $1.1 trillion in 2018.
- The app store revenue was $92.1 billion in 2018.[11]

Interesting Smartphone Trivia

- In Seoul, South Korea, the number of smartphone-involved traffic accidents has tripled over the last five years.

- In Germany, there are traffic lights on the ground for distracted phone users.
- In China, there are designated lanes for "petextrians" created especially for cell phone users.
- In Finland, there is an annual "mobile phone throwing" championship.[12]

Self-Generated Sexual Material by Teens (aged 13–17)

- 27% of kids (aged 9–17) and 40% of kids (aged 13–17) agreed that "it's normal for people my age to share nudes with each other."
- 20% (1 in 5) kids believe it is okay to share a nude as long as you send it over an app that doesn't save it.
- 56% of kids have shared nudes through a secondary account their parents are not aware of.
- On some platforms, kids are more likely to have their accounts set to public than set to private. (This may be due to an effort to acquire "followers and likes.")
- 47% of kids who have shared nudes report feeling positive following the experience, while 36% report feeling shame and guilt.
- 33% (1 in 3) kids reported sharing a nude with someone they had not met.
- Parents are waiting to have the conversation until kids get older. Among parents who have NOT had a conversation with their child regarding Self-Gen-

erated Sexual Material, 31% have kids in high school, 40% have kids in middle school and 51% have kids in elementary school.

Pornography Internet Statistics

- About half of 8th graders have viewed pornography.[13]
- Pornography is most often accessed through cell phones.[14]
- 84.4% of males (ages 14–18) and 57% of females (ages 14–18) have viewed pornography.[15]
- 29% of male 10th graders have seen violent pornography.
- 16% of female 10th graders have seen violent pornography.[16]
- 71% of teens come across internet porn without even looking for it.
- 29% of internet sex crimes relationships were initiated on a social networking site.
- 33% of all internet sex crimes involved social networking sites.
- In 26% of online sex crimes against minors, offenders disseminated information and/or pictures of the victim through the victim's personal social networking site.
- 67% of teens say they know how to hide what they do online from their parents.
- 39% think their online activity is private from everyone, including their parents.

- 55% have given out information, including photos and personal descriptions, to someone they don't know.
- 29% have been stalked or contacted by someone they don't know.[17]

Now the Disturbing Stats

- According to data from the SEMrush Traffic Analytics tool, porn sites received more website traffic in 2020 than Twitter, Instagram, Netflix, Zoom, Pinterest, and LinkedIn combined (SEMrush).[18]
- 21.7 million reports of suspected child sexual exploitation were made to the Cyber Tipline (2020) an increase of 28% from 2019.[19]
- Tech companies reported over 45 million online photos and videos of children being sexually abused (2019).[20]
- 1 in 10 children 10 years old and younger account for 22% of all online obscene content consumption in the 18-years-old-and-under category (2019).[21]
- 50% of all internet traffic is related to sex.[22]
- 2.5 billion emails sent or received every day contain porn (US stat).[23]
- Every 39 minutes a new pornography video is being created in the US.[24]
- 47 million porn videos are viewed by 7–14-year-olds in the US every day.[25]
- National survey says 64% (ages 13–24) actively seek out porn weekly or more often.[26]

- 82 million porn videos are viewed daily by children (globally).[27]
- In 2016, people watched 4.6 billion hours of pornography.[28]
- 80% of 15–17-year-olds have had multiple exposures to hardcore **XXX** material.[29]

Something to Note

"The other unprecedented characteristic of pornography is the ease in which children and adolescents have access to it—both solicited and unsolicited access. In the past, the adult bookstore or restricted movie theatre was a tangible gatekeeper or buffer to minors being exposed to material. Currently, anyone can be a consumer and or target of sexually explicit material."[30] —*Jill C. Manning, 2007*

Conclusion

No doubt internet and social media statistics could fill terabytes of storage, easily overwhelming the novice interpreter. Grappling with multiple layers of data in an effort to construct a basic summary emerges as a monumental task, leaving one exhausted. Many of these statistics are used for creating marketing and advertising strategies to intentionally track the current trends of targeted age groups, drawing conclusions from the direction of popular culture.

Regardless of the ability to manipulate information toward an end goal in an effort to effect a specific outcome, there are three conclusions an individual can reasonably draw.

The first conclusion readily formed is the heavy use of mobile devices, the internet, and social media platforms worldwide. Technology has infiltrated familial life and changed the very fabric of daily routines for billions of people. This is obviously not a trend; this is now a way of life. One example would be the disappearance of the landline in the home. House phones have been replaced by our mobile phones. "So what?" you might ask. Think about the following: before mobile devices, if someone wanted to speak to one of your children, they had to call the home telephone number and pass the parental sniff test. Parents were aware of who was calling, how often, and how long the conversations lasted because the telephone was a shared device within a home. In the simple act of a parent answering the phone, considerable information could be gained regarding the company their child keeps. This interaction has been replaced with our children privately texting or taking calls often without our knowledge. An important parental tool silently slipped away and hardly anyone noticed.

This example can be expanded further. Not so long ago, it was considered necessary and polite for a teen to greet their friend at the front door of the family home before heading out for the evening. Most parents deemed honking a car horn from the driveway an inconsiderate and unacceptable form of notification of one's arrival. With the expectation of friends walking to the front door and ringing the doorbell, a parent received another opportunity to hold their child and friends accountable for pending plans. This ritual has been replaced with a muted text from the friend who sits in their car parked in your driveway.

With basic observation skills, a reasonable person can competently reach the second conclusion. It is not so much about the statistics, but more about what kids have access to. There is no denying the dizzying pace in which social media and internet statistics change. Solid information gained less than one year ago can be radically different in real time. I found myself running in circles attempting to stay current with the rapidly changing platforms, only to discover the scope of their ability to morph. It became apparent to me; I was only providing band-aid solutions. The sheer volume and speed in which this industry creates, transforms, and evolves presents a serious management challenge for most parents.

The final conclusion, not to be underestimated, points a glaring spotlight squarely on the economics of the industry itself. It is simply mind-boggling to note a mobile ecosystem created less than thirty years ago has exploded into a global trillion-dollar business. In one form or another, billions of people participate in the continued financial success of the internet and social media platforms. This includes all things good, bad, and ugly. Make no mistake, the porn industry claims an impressive share of the economic pie.

Despite the endless rich rewards of internet advances, I remained steadfastly focused in my pursuit to educate my daughter regarding her secretive adolescent activities on the World Wide Web. It was mandatory I peel back the layers of what she termed harmless superficial fun and expose what lay beneath the surface.

In an effort to make an impactful impression, I intentionally zeroed in on statistics on the dark web where the porn industry lurks, searching for the most horrifying data I could find. In truth, the data was alarming, but perhaps more disturbing was what I ultimately discovered. Child pornography is a global multi-billion-dollar industry that one does not need to go in search of. This criminal element will meet your child on any public platform they are given access to. This revelation jolted me to another level of reality.

Internet porn has infiltrated every corner of the web. The ability to view porn any place, anytime has revolutionized the industry. Those who desire to contact and entrap our children by exposing them to porn have infinite opportunities to do just that.

The most obvious exposure starts with social media accounts without privacy blocks, and extends to interactive gaming platforms and chat rooms. Additionally, there is the YouTube video recommendation feed that continuously suggests your next viewing option. Finally, the more subtle pop-up ads* and clickbait links** relentlessly appear as an unsolicited suggestion alongside a news or sports feed. Both work endlessly to capture your curiosity

*Pop-up ads are forms of online advertising. A pop-up is a graphical user interface display area, usually a small window, that suddenly appears in the foreground of the visual interface.

and lure you from your intended task. The scope of possibilities is endless, but one thing is for certain: like a chameleon, it frequently changes colors to meet you where you are.

The critical challenge for most parents is the ability to stay consistent and vigilant in keeping track of not only their children's use of technology, but also the pace and speed of technological advances. Often, it proves to be an overwhelming task, complicating and testing our adeptness to parent our children in the modern world.

**Clickbait is a text or thumbnail link that is designed to attract attention and entice users to follow that link and read, view, or listen to the content online. Clickbait has a defining characteristic of being deceptive, typically sensationalized or misleading. (Wikipedia)

Fifteen

Understanding Social Media and the Psychology Behind It

I had never given much thought to the creation and development of social media . . . until now.

I would argue there are very few people who have not heard of Facebook. Created in 2004 with 2.8 billion users worldwide at the end of 2020, Facebook continues to be a front-runner in social media platforms.[31] However, before there was a Facebook, there was SixDegrees, one of the original pioneers of social platforms followed by Myspace. If I am being honest, I had never heard of SixDegrees and I can barely recall Myspace, although it lurks in my distant memory. These social media platforms were born with the advent of the internet and caught fire in less than a twenty-year time span. They were designed to connect people. Mission accomplished. We now have the first generation that does not know life prior to the internet and social media. Having been born into a world where this technology already exists, Generation Z often views their devices as an extension of their world.[32]

In my universe, I often felt my daily encounters were mostly of interest to only a select few, that being my husband and maybe my kids if I was lucky. Admittedly, my experience with social media was limited. I mean, who really cares what happened on my way to the grocery store? Instead, I found myself more enamored with the ability to use maps and occasionally check on the whereabouts of my children. But obviously not everyone feels the same.

Having said that, it is difficult not to notice the delight others take in checking their Facebook or Instagram feed. With diverted eyes locked in place, thumbs consistently swipe screens upward in a rhythmic motion for the next bit of news frequently followed by spontaneous laughter or an unintentional gasp. Sound familiar? Often, what is on that tiny little cell phone screen appears to have more power than any other person in the room. The captivation of social media cannot be denied. Each notification ping is answered with an involuntary reaction from the consumer to satisfy the need to check the alert. Distraction is almost certainly a given when a smartphone is present, sometimes to the point of complete oblivion to one's physical surroundings.

It would appear that people do not want to be separated from their various forms of technology, myself included. It feels like a lifeline that should not be left behind when you venture out into the world.

So, what is it about technology and all the appendages that have placed such a powerful stronghold on people in modern-day society?

What Is the Psychology Behind Social Media?

"We can now create machines that can change what people think and what people do, and the machines can do that autonomously."[33] —*Dr. B. J. Fogg, Stanford University*

Who Is Dr. B. J. Fogg?

- A psychologist and father of persuasive technology
- Created the Fogg Behavior Model
- Researcher and Professor at Stanford University
- Stanford Professor to Mike Krieger (cofounder of Instagram)
- Director of Persuasive Technology Lab at Stanford
- Architect of contemporary communication methods

What Is Persuasive Technology?

A discipline in which digital machines and apps (including smartphones, social media, and video games) are configured to alter human thoughts and behaviors.

What Is the Fogg Behavior Model?

The well-tested method to change behavior in its simplified form involves three primary factors: Motivation, Ability, and Triggers. This formula is the blueprint widely credited for building multibillion-dollar social media and gaming companies.

How It Works according to Fogg

- *Motivator*: the user's desire for "social acceptance" or the desire "to avoid being socially rejected" rooted in three core motivators (sensation, anticipation, and belonging).
- *Ability*: digital products are designed so that the user does not have to think hard. Social networks are easy to navigate.
- *Trigger*: endless notifications, numerous digital tricks to urge you to constantly check your phone for new information. After you have been triggered enough, it becomes internalized.

Fogg Model in Action Using Snapchat

- *Motivator*: You feel like you belong by connecting with friends, there is anticipation of seeing new and unexpected content and finally the sensations you feel when viewing content (happy, sad, etc.).
- *Ability*: It is simple to use and it is empowering (creating with filters etc.).
- *Trigger*: Notifications and pings trigger the action for you to check.

Why It Works

Persuasive technologies work because of their ability to trigger the release of dopamine, a powerful neurotransmitter which controls reward, attention, and addiction.

In addiction, variable reward (a brain manipulation technique) is used. The user stays engaged waiting for the next "like" or "game reward."

Behind the development and use of this tech model are countless psychologists, neuroscientists, and social science experts working to devise products that capture and keep the consumer's attention. Users are purposefully targeted through digital environments that are manipulated to fulfill their basic human drives (to be social and obtain goals).

Who Are "They"?

- Ramsay Brown, founder of Dopamine Labs: "We have now developed a rigorous technology of the mind. And around the world hundreds of thousands of people are going to quietly change their behavior in ways that, unbeknownst to them, feel second nature but are really by design."
- Facebook executives internal report: ". . . by monitoring posts, interactions, and photos in real time, we have the ability to micro-target ads down to the moment when young people need a confidence boost."
- John Hopson (PhD in behavioral and brain sci-

ence) was hired by Microsoft to help lead the development of Xbox Live. In his paper "Behavioral Game Design," Hopson gives an explanation of how psychology is used in game design to maintain player interests by asking the following questions, "How do we make players maintain a high, consistent rate of activity?" and "How to make players play forever?"

- Bill Fulton (trained in cognitive and quantitative psychology), founder of Microsoft's Games User-Research group: "If game designers are going to pull a person away from every other voluntary social activity or hobby or pastime, they're going to have to engage the person at a very deep level in every possible way they can."

The result is a billion-dollar industry with a side effect of addiction.

Those Sounding the Alarm

- Tristan Harris, formerly a design ethicist at Google: "The job of these companies is to hook people, and they do that by hijacking our psychological vulnerabilities."
- Sean Parker, former Facebook president: "The thought process that went into building applications was all about how do we consume as much of your time and conscious attention as possible."[34]
- Marc Benioff, CEO Salesforce (a cloud comput-

ing company): "Technology has addictive qualities that we have to address, and that product designers are working to make those products more addictive, and we need to rein that back as much as possible."[35]

The Takeaway

- Persuasive technology is the secret sauce in the development of social media, apps, gaming, and the internet.

- Apps give you the illusion of free choice, but the pathway has already been set with predetermined choices.

- Much of what we do online releases dopamine into the brain's pleasure centers, creating a cycle of repetitive desire and need.

- The release of dopamine forms the basis for addiction.

- Tech companies actively design media in order to keep users addicted or obsessed.

- "Gaming companies talk openly about creating a 'compulsion loop.'"[36]

- "In the past, society has been able to put physical barriers in place to make it more difficult to satisfy unhealthy obsessions."[37] There are no longer any physical barriers because the smartphone is portable.

Conclusion

I will admit, I had a lightning bolt moment after reading the definition of Persuasive Technology and the subsequent strategy outlined in the Fogg model. At first glance, I mistakenly concluded the use of the word "persuasive" as a process meant to appeal to reason or understanding through a convincing exchange between several individuals.

However, upon closer inspection, it became evident to me that the techniques used in Persuasive Technology are masterfully created and utilized with a very specific result in mind. I was stunned to notice the clear absence of choice. The discipline based on the Fogg model is designed to alter human thoughts and behaviors, not to present options.

This knowledge instantly expanded my ability to understand the younger generation and their attachment to digital devices, further allowing me to make sense of my daughter's relationship with social media.

As a parent, an indisputable turning point occurred which proved to be unavoidable. Social media and gaming platforms are intentionally designed with the goal of embedding and ultimately addicting (yes, I said it) its loyal participants. There is no way around it, that is the end game.

With an onslaught of emotions, I felt like I had discovered the secret sauce behind the hypnotic power of interactive media. Every parent who passively or intentionally places a digital device in their child's hand should have complete knowledge and understanding of the psychologists, neuroscientists, and social science experts who work so diligently to create and perpetuate this seemingly harmless technology into our lives and those of our loved ones.

Sixteen

How Technology Impacts the Brain

As a mother of one teenager and two grown children, I have enough ongoing experience to judge the following to be true:

It only makes sense that repeated actions lead to habits which, in turn, define behavior.

We can trust our common sense to determine this. We can also trust our eyes to know what we see and our ears to know what we hear. It does not take a licensed genius to conclude things have changed drastically from when we were kids. We only need to be observant.

Let's face it, our kids are easily distracted, often becoming impatient with a conversation that lasts more than ten minutes. It is not unusual to find them sitting in front of the television while simultaneously skimming their phone. If they are comfortable with us, they will casually broach edgy subjects using phrases and words that in the past would have only been reserved for their peers.

Some of our kids are so anxiety ridden and socially fragile, schools have created "safe spaces." What does this really say about us as a society? Are we more compassionate people than in the past, or have we lost common decency toward others? Or as parents, did we fail to teach basic life skills to our kids?

They problem-solve at an accelerated rate, using the internet to access necessary information. They expertly retrieve phone numbers, get directions and locate the nearest Starbucks, all in a matter of minutes. But they do not know how to read a map, independently solve a problem, properly spell, or write in cursive.

No doubt, the cyber world in which we live has affected how we interact with each other. That is a foregone conclusion. More in-depth contemplation would lead one to consider how our brains have and are evolving into something much different than in the past.

When the Brain and Technology Collide

"While much of the technology we are senselessly addicted to promises us greater connectedness, people are more isolated, disconnected and lonely, than ever before in history."[38] —*Bryant H. McGill, author*

Technology in the Classroom

- 86% of educators use laptops in the classroom.
- 58% use educational apps.

- 47% of teachers say they are embracing social media to collaborate with other teachers.
- 25% of teachers indicate they are intimidated by students' use and knowledge of tech.
- Some schools are providing only online textbooks.
- Most schools require assignments to be submitted electronically.
- Homework assignments are posted electronically.
- Grades are posted electronically.
- Greater course offerings and resources for both students and teachers. [39]

What's really going on in the classroom according to Joe Clement and Matt Miles, authors of *Screen Schooled:*

- Heavy use of technology has impacted students' cognitive abilities.
- Distracted kids are showing little intellectual curiosity and poor problem-solving skills.
- Incapable of deeper or creative thought.
- Students struggle to make basic connections & think beyond anything concrete.
- Students are easily entranced by screen time and become more disengaged from class, teachers and even each other.
- Decreased ability to retain knowledge.
- Decreased ability to stay focused for a longer period of time.
- Critical thinking skills affected.

- In-classroom social skills decreased.[40]

"By providing easily obtained answers to any conceivable question, young people have grown to over-rely on these devices to do the thinking for them."[41] —Screen Schooled: Two Veteran Teachers Expose How Technology Overuse Is Making Our Kids Dumber

The Impact

How frequent internet use affects brain functioning:

- **Concentration** - the stream of online information demands attention across multiple media sources (hyperlinks, notifications, and prompts). Also known as "media multitasking."
- **Memory** - vast amounts of information are quickly available and retrievable. Because information is so easy to obtain, there is no need to offload through books, friends, or community.
- **Information** - the internet is clearly changing the way we store, retrieve, and value knowledge.
- **Social cognition** - social media platforms can resemble real-world social processes. They are able to directly quantify acceptance and rejection through "friends, followers, and likes." This presents an enormous change in the rules of social interaction.
- **Critical thinking** - is facilitated by information that is stored in our long-term memory. Basically,

it is how all the dots get connected.[42]

"Neuro-imaging of frequent internet users shows twice as much activity in the short-term memory as sporadic users during online tasks. Basically, our brain is learning to disregard information found online, and this connection becomes stronger every time we experience it."[43]

Social Media and Mental Health

Three billion people visit multiple social media platforms a day.[44]

- **Self-esteem and confidence** - many social media platforms focus on appearance and show-casing a fulfilling and exciting life. Reality is easily altered through lighting and filters. Viewing others' selfies often results in comparing yourself to an altered image, triggering emotions such as envy and jealousy.

- **Depression** - there is a link between social media and depression. Symptoms can intensify, including a decrease in social activity and increase in feelings of loneliness.

- **Sleep** - the artificial lighting, especially the blue light emitted by smartphone, tablets and laptop screens, can inhibit the production of melatonin (the hormone that helps you sleep). The bright light can delay circadian rhythms necessary for sleep. There are also the pings and need to check for social media updates. Sleep loss for teens can result in: moodiness, drop in grades, overeating, tiredness, lowered immune system, and irritability.

- **Relationships** - a smartphone presence can interfere with social interactions between people, especially during conversations about something meaningful. It goes without saying how this might happen. Facebook can affect how an individual feels about the quality of their own relationships, especially romantic ones.[45]

- **Envy and jealousy** - the comparison game can quickly lead to strong feelings of envy and jealousy; the unfortunate by-product is sometimes cyberbullying and mean behavior.[46]

- **Anxiety** - teens who are invested in their social media accounts often feel more pressure to respond quickly, have perfect photos, and to craft clever and well-written responses. There is also pressure to keep up with the unwritten rules and culture of the platform.

- **Communication issues** - communicating online does not lend itself to seeing a person's facial expression or hearing someone's tone of voice. Non-verbal cues are missed. All of the above can easily lead to misunderstandings.[47]

- **Emotional well-being** - social media has been linked to stimulating the emotions of jealousy, envy, and loneliness.[48]

- **Social isolation** - research has found those who spend the most amount of time on social media are two times more likely to experience social isolation. They also experience a sense of loss in belonging and missed opportunities to build meaningful relationships with others. They are more likely to have a distorted view of other people's lives.
- **Social media addiction** - has not yet been officially classified as an addiction. The Netherlands has classified Internet addiction as an addiction disorder.[49]

Porn's Impact on the Brain

This is what the scientific community says:

- "Teens and preteens with highly plastic brains are compulsively using high speed Internet porn with their porn taste becoming out of sync with their real-life sexuality."[50]
- A 2015 study by the Journal of Sex Research states that: "Constant novelty and primacy of sexual stimuli as a particularly strong natural reward makes Internet pornography a unique activator of the brain's reward system" and "novelty is compelling because it triggers a burst of dopamine in regions of the brain strongly associated with reward and goal-directed behavior."[51]
- Researchers believe that pornography's intense stimulation of the brain brings about significant

changes in the brain, similar to drug addiction.

- Researchers have found a correlation between brain activity and age—the younger the age, the greater level of activity in the ventral striatum of the brain in response to pornography.
- Those with compulsive sexual behavior have brain activity that mirrors those of drug addicts.
- As hours of reported pornography use increases, the amount of gray matter in the brain decreases.[52]
- "When you give people immediate access to highly stimulating, highly pleasurable content or experiences the likelihood that addiction will appear goes up."[53]

Conclusion

Technology has firmly established its place in the classroom, altering the way our children learn and take in information. The recent events of Covid-19 have driven our students deeper online.

With the increased reliance upon the computer by educators and students alike, how cognitive skills evolve and learning takes place has been affected. Few would dispute this, recognizing in students a lack of creative thinking, difficulty with abstract thinking, decreased ability to retain information, and an inability to think concretely.

When faced with a problem in need of a solution, our children are resourceful with the use of the internet, or more specifically a YouTube tutorial, to identify and resolve a problem quickly. Take that ability away from them and see what happens. Do they know where to start, how to figure it out, how to gain resources? Do they know who and how to ask?

At one time or another, each of my children have asked how I gained information before the internet. They were curious and perplexed, wondering how I conducted research for a school paper. The easy answer was I accessed the school or local library using microfiche and their card catalogue system. Their questions continued with: How did I learn to change a tire and what did I use before Google maps? Again, the answer was rather simple: Someone taught or helped me. I also learned how to read a map. If all else failed, I sat there until I figured it out.

The advantage of a smartphone most definitely eliminates frustration by providing quick answers and easy directions to almost any imaginable question or unfamiliar task. The instant access to information also conserves time, a commodity most of us value.

Consider the following: the ability to tap the internet for information on the as-needed basis has affected student's cognitive ability and long-term memory. They experience little need to retain data that is so easily accessible, potentially resulting in a depleted bank of personal knowledge.

While technological gadgets have enriched our lives, it has also indirectly taken something from us as a society. Specifically, it has eliminated a dynamic opportunity to learn. It has deprived us of an opening to connect in person and without technology to another human being through a common interest or need. A gateway to appreciate and value another person's ability or skill set that subtly provided a segue into another human being's life has disappeared. Perhaps most importantly, such circumstances could often provide an opportunity for an individual to gain self-confidence and self-esteem. The former mentioned being in short supply as evidenced by much of our youths' depression and anxiety.

While the classroom is one venue where our children learn, the playground, now replaced by mobile devices, is the other. Social media is at the center of how most young people conduct and manage the many dynamics of their lives. The gamut is covered through endless online games, forms of entertainment, ways to communicate and showcase talents. In addition, infinite platforms are available for social, cultural, and political commentaries. Our children readily become smitten with the possibilities of a customized virtual world that allows them to control the many aspects of their universe. The absence of face-to-face interaction comes with heavy consequences. So, what are we missing? Remember when commentary on a literal playground typically was solicited or invited? At best, it was an opportunity for a meaningful exchange of thoughts and ideas, an addition into your bank of knowledge and experience. At worst, an exchange might provoke posturing, possibly resulting in a disagreement and parting of ways. In an ideal world, the playground provided an exercise in tolerance and compromise. Regardless of all possible outcomes, one way or another it was settled on the playground, face-to-face.

Many would argue digital devices have given us the ability to connect with others, but oddly enough the opposite is true. With the convenience and popularity of digital connection comes a sacrifice of subtle nonverbal cues that people experience and often rely on during face-to-face communication. For example, the implied message sent by a slightly raised eyebrow could make the difference between someone proceeding with a dialogue or ending the conversation. With a void of energy in the room, inability to read body language, and a lack of natural verbal exchanges, many of us misinterpret the exchange and often end up being misunderstood.

In a virtual safe space, which ironically is anything but safe, our kids can and do further create their own reality. This ability to customize interests and more specifically "your world" is actually divisive. I believe it takes away a critical skill set to consider things (people and ideas) outside of the comfort of your created world. Remember, social media has AI ability (Artificial Intelligence), * therefore recognizing and continually feeding you what you agree with and more importantly are comfortable with. It is simply a cycle of reinforcement for the interests and convictions you already have. Why do you think an item or service you recently viewed online keeps popping up?

As a parent, all of these topics are concerning.

*Artificial Intelligence - The theory and development of computer systems able to perform tasks that normally require human intelligence, such as visual perception, speech recognition, and decision making.

But for me, the most horrifying and alarming issue is the impact pornographic visual material has on the brain. Whether a kid stumbled upon it, sought it out, or was targeted by an online predator, the initial result is the same, the exposure has occurred. You cannot unsee what you just saw.

The current research provides answers while at the same time creating more questions. It is clear viewing pornography activates the brain's natural reward system. Research shows the more porn is used as a stimulant, the more difficult it becomes to change the behavior, setting the individual up for an addictive component.

These are the questions I am still seeking answers to:

- How is the brain impacted when a young child views hard-core porn while neurons and mirror neurons are activated?
- What happens when a young child is consistently exposed to graphic internet porn and they have no ability to process what they have seen due to an undeveloped frontal cortex?
- Is an addictive behavior now in place?
- Are secondary reactionary behaviors now in place?
- Does this mean the child has experienced trauma?
- Can the trauma be undone?

Millions of children in the United States as well as around the world have experienced this very trauma.

Something more to consider: If the internet has an AI

component, every time a pornographic website is viewed, the computer registers this and continues to present visited material to the individual. This becomes a type of virtual quicksand, creating entrapment that young people find difficult to break free of.

Seventeen

Online Behaviors and Associated Risks

I have always revered one of Dr. Phil's most famous quotes: "You choose the behavior; you choose the consequences."[54] Wow! I love this because it does not get more bottom line than that. It is crystal clear. As a young mother, I tucked this "Phil-ism" into my toolbox of parenting skills under parental wisdom.

Over the years, the philosophy served me well, especially when my children were young and the stakes were relatively low. But with the advent of the internet and more specifically the smartphone, turning these words into action became a different story. In practice, allowing my children to suffer the natural consequences of their social media actions became downright dangerous, coupled with the potential for terrible results. Those stakes were too high and flew in the face of my better judgment and mother bear instincts. Little did I know how insightful that observation would turn out to be.

Parenthood hit me like a ton of bricks. From the moment I held each of my babies in my arms, I was overwhelmed with a sense of responsibility to protect, nurture, love, and spiritually guide these little beings to the best of my ability. The work at hand was not to shape them in my exact image, but rather discover who they were uniquely destined to be and provide guidance toward their best version. It was a clear yet daunting task. Their souls were placed in my hands and I felt privileged to be their mother. I was and still am dead serious about that.

This was equally true in 2003 when my youngest daughter was born. Many things had changed in the seven years since there had been a baby in the house. My daughter was fiery, curious, smart, and technologically savvy. By the time she was five years old, our house was filled with smartphones, iPads, laptops, game stations, and teenagers.

In full disclosure, I did not see the perfect storm brewing on the horizon. However, I would ultimately learn the following: in the world of social media, every choice reflecting poor judgment is a potential black hole to fall into with diminishing hope of recovery.

The Physical and Emotional Cost of Technology

"You choose the behavior, you choose the consequences."
—*Dr. Phil*

I. SEXTING - the electronic sharing of sexually explicit images, video, or messages.

- At least 1 in 4 teens (ages 12–17) receive sexually explicit texts.
- At least 1 in 7 are sending sexts.
- More than 1 in 10 teens are forwarding sexts without consent.
- About 1 in 12 have had sexts they have sent or forwarded without consent.[55]

Unintended Consequences of Sexting

- **No control over who sends and receives** - Sexts get forwarded over and over again. There is no such thing as a "secret" on social media.

- **Emotional fallout** - feelings of guilt, shame, embarrassment and humiliation.

- **Bullying and harassment** - compromising sexts or pictures can be held against you in a multitude of ways.

- **Boundaries pushed** - some may see how far you will go by asking for more sexts, pics, etc.

- **Bad mistakes** - easy to send the wrong message to the wrong person.

- **Destroying your reputation** - it only takes one picture, one sext.

- **Messed-up view of relationships** - direct human-to-human interactions can never be replaced by electronic communication.

- **Legal ramification** - most of the sexting involves minors, therefore nude photos are legally considered child pornography regardless of who is sending.[56]

II. SMARTPHONE - a device that combines a cell phone with a handheld computer, typically offering internet access and data storage.

- Average age to receive a smartphone is 10.
- Ability to connect to social media platforms.
- Smartphones are a two-way device: you can send and receive.
- Use of apps makes information trackable.
- Smartphones are the keepers of memories (camera, video, birthday texts).[57]

Unintended Consequences of Smartphones

- Person (known or unknown) on the receiving end can misuse or abuse information.
- Stalking or being stalked.
- Ignoring or being ignored.
- Receiving unwanted sexual solicitation.
- Lost communication skills (the ability to speak to others, think, and communicate spontaneously, translate non-verbals, the ability to be focused on others, communicating with authenticity, interacting face-to-face, the ability and desire to listen, the ability to build an argument).[58]

III. SOCIAL PLATFORMS - web-based technologies that enable the development, deployment, and management of social media solutions and services (Facebook, Instagram, Snapchat, YouTube).

Benefits of Social Media

- Staying connected to family and friends.
- Shared interests with others.
- Finding community.
- Identifying others with common interests.
- Creating business.
- Public message sharing.[59]

Unintended Consequences of Social Platforms

- Loss of growing up and making mistakes in private.[60]
- Identity theft.[61]
- College admissions potentially compromised.[62]
- Employment opportunities potentially compromised.
- Humiliating or publicly shaming others with potential legal ramifications.[63]
- Personal relationships potentially compromised.
- Easy to be mean or cruel.[64]

IV. THE SELFIE - a photograph one has taken of oneself with a smartphone or webcam and shared via social media.

- 259 deaths have been reported as a result of taking selfies (October 2011–November 2017).
- The highest number of selfie-deaths have been reported in India, with the US in third place.
- Selfies are never reported as an official cause of death, therefore they are more than likely under-reported.
- "No selfie zones" have been established in popular tourist areas (in particular bodies of water, cliffs, mountain peaks and tall buildings).[65]
- The Louvre has established a 60-second rule in front of the *Mona Lisa* as a result of people taking selfies.[66]
- There are selfie museums in major cities around the world.
- 24 billion selfies were uploaded to Google in 2015.
- 1 million selfies are clicked on in a day.[67]

Unintended Consequences of Selfies

- Increased feeling of depression, anxiety, poor body image, and loneliness.
- Lower ability and confidence to take risks.[68]
- Narcissistic behavior and tendencies.
- Giving your power of self-worth to other individuals through the calculable results of "likes."
- Lower self-esteem.
- Image over identity.
- Unattainable comparisons to peers or strangers.

- Oversexualized poses and clothing.[69]
- Death.

V. YOUTUBE - a video-sharing service that allows viewers to watch, like, comment and share videos posted by others and upload their own videos.

2020 statistics

- 2 billion monthly active users.
- 30 million daily active users.
- 5+ billion videos shared to date.
- 1 billion mobile YouTube views per day.
- 70% viewer watch time comes from mobile devices.
- 95% of the global internet population watches YouTube.
- 85% of teens use YouTube (2018).
- 500 hours of viewing content are uploaded per minute.[70]

Unintended Consequences of YouTube

- Perpetrators have manipulated content to target youth.
- Easy for kids to stumble upon inappropriate sexual video clips specifically targeted to them.
- Exposure leads to kids acting out sexually.
- Easy to follow or subscribe to YouTube content. As

a result, you are subject to whatever content that user creates and pushes to the subscriber.[71] Big deal? Think about it!

VI. SNAPCHAT - Mobile app and service for sharing photos, videos and messages with other people that disappear once the recipient reads them.

- There are ways to capture and recover images that allegedly disappear.
- Snap Map (2017) allows users to share their location in real time with anyone.
- Discover feature (2015) allows you to see content from popular media channels (often sexually oriented).
- Snapstreak - when users "snap" back and forth within a twenty-four-hour period for three days. Rewarded with a flame emoji and number next to streakers' names.[72]

Impulsive Actions and Risky Behavior Pave the Road to Regrets and Big Trouble

- Posting party pics/video.
- Posting illegal activity.
- Posting personal pictures/video in over-sexualized clothing.
- Humiliating or publicly shaming others.

- Viral video attempts.[73]
- Oversharing personal information.[74]
- Viewing inappropriate content.[75]
- Creating inappropriate content.[76]
- Desire to get extreme and unusual selfie pics to post on social media.[77]
- The seeking of attention and validation through selfies.
- Using social media "likes" for validation.
- Obsessive behavior in creating the perfect image.[78]
- Being oblivious to things going on around you, literally.[79]

Conclusion

Anyone who has children knows: good decisions and kids do not always go together. Bad decisions are going to happen.

When kids live life online, their choices are often irreparable and magnified for the whole world to see. The moment the send button is pushed, control has been given up. This certainly may sound dire and extreme, but it is the truth. It is commonly assumed online communications are private and respected, especially amongst friends, but that is not always the case. Oftentimes kids simply do not have the ability or life experience to fully realize all potential risks and consequences. What often begins as innocent fun or curiosity can frequently lead to risky behavior ending in unintended consequences.

Why is this?

The frontal cortex of the brain, responsible for judgment, impulse control, social and sexual behavior, is not fully developed until around the age of twenty-five. With never-ending access to social media and an ability to post anytime and anywhere, we should not be shocked when a child impulsively makes a decision that turns out to be irreversible. When we hand our children tech devices, we are allowing them to play with fire. Even with close supervision, we still gamble on the relationship we have with our children and their willingness to seek us out when they get in over their heads.

To be straightforward, there are few ways to create complete protected isolation from mistakes made online. Therefore, one must depend upon cultivating the parent-child relationship and expanding the education around technology provided to our children. They are all at risk, and it is our job to try and minimize that risk to the best of our ability.

The fact of the matter is, in the world of technology, forgiveness and grace are nonexistent. Many of us have painfully experienced or witnessed the abysmal absence of re-dos or un-dos, some of which have ultimately altered the course of our lives. Unfortunately, there is no magic eraser.

Whether you are the villain or the victim, the hunter or the hunted, the end result is the same: someone gets hurt. The damage is more than a permanent scar on a knee or an embarrassing moment in time; it is a wound to the very psyche of someone's soul. It becomes a defining moment in how the rest of the world sees an individual and as a result, how they see themselves. Herein lies the potential to shatter a human life.

In another time, indiscretions were the war stories of our youth we shared as adults. Often it would be one person's word against another. Being found in a compromising position may at best stir hurtful rumors, at worst damage your reputation. Either way, with the benefit of time, the possibility still existed to find an opportunity for reinvention. These are the promises of yesterday; gone are the black-and-white answers of raising children in a technology-rich world.

Eighteen

Tech Giants and Their Children

I believe 100% in personal responsibility, but I must admit, this one gets to me.

As I began to expand my education surrounding social media, my curiosity quickly turned to the people who created and developed these platforms. I became acutely interested in their personal opinions. Furthermore, I was intensely focused on the parameters and restrictions they place on their own children. I was surprised to discover the depth of information related to this pursuit and astonished by the candor in which they addressed the subject matter.

In an effort to step back and put things into perspective, I reasoned the following: just because you manufacture alcohol does not mean you drink it yourself or allow your children to. This is a solid statement, but there is a notable difference between alcohol and technology. The shared education regarding technology is not there. In addition, there is a moral component missing.

Make no mistake, there is a double standard for the children whose parents work and live in Silicon Valley. Look closely at the schools their children attend. Look closer at their actions regarding their children and usage of technology. Clearly, decisions were based on information.

The collective conscience of the people who created social media and gaming platforms went straight out the door the minute we started drinking the Kool-Aid. Shame on them. Shame on me.

In our urban household, education was a top priority. Private schools touting the latest technology in the classroom were absolutely the necessary path to the top universities in the country. In fact, it was required. How fortunate we were to grab hold of the future. The promise of protection from the Wild West of the internet was built into the laptop standards established by the high school. With smart boards in every classroom, grades and communications online, we enthusiastically took our place at the table.

What Do the Tech Giants Actually Do?

"You look around the restaurants and pretty much everyone has their phone on the table and they're just being constantly drawn away from the live face-to-face interaction—I do think that's a bad thing."[80] —*Dr. B. J. Fogg*

- **Steve Jobs**, CEO of Apple until his death in

2012, prohibited his children from using the newly released iPad.

- **Bill Gates**, Microsoft founder, banned smartphones at the table, placed time limits on screen time, did not provide kids a phone until fourteen years of age, and allowed no tech in the bedroom.

- **Tim Cook**, Current Apple CEO, does not allow his nephew to join online social networks and has stated, "Apple products are not meant for constant use."[81]

- **Susan Hobbs**, Chief of Staff at Cloudflare, completely banned her daughter from social media until age sixteen.[82]

- **Chris Anderson**, founder of Wired, CEO of 3D Robotics, said, "With 5 kids, all tech in the house has parental controls. We have seen the dangers of technology firsthand. I don't want to see that happen to my kids."[83]

- **Evan Williams**, cofounder of Twitter, Medium, and Blogger - He and his wife have "amassed a collection of books" in lieu of digital tech products to help their two sons become more well-read."[84]

- **Athena Chavarria**, former Facebook executive assistant, Chan Zuckerberg Initiative: "I am convinced the devil lives in our phones and is wreaking havoc on our children."[85]

- **John Lilly**, former CEO of Mozilla: "I keep trying to tell him somebody wrote code to make you feel this way—I'm trying to help him understand how things are made, the values that are going into things and what people are doing to create that feeling." Lilly's attempt to educate his son on what appears to be harmless fun (tech) is actually a manipulation.[86]

- **Taewoo Kim**, chief AI engineer One Smart Lab: ". . . you can't put your face in a device and expect to develop a long-term attention span."[87]

- **Vijay Koduri**, former Google employee, currently developing HashCut - Vijay banned video game systems in his household, does not give children cell phones, and only allows them to play games on the parents' phones for ten minutes per week.[88]

How Tech Giants Educate Their Children

Waldorf School

- School philosophy: Interaction between students and their teachers (ages 3–14 or through 8th grade) must be the priority. It is more important to work with real materials than to interface with the electronic media or technology.[89]

- Computers and screens are not allowed in the classroom.[90]

- Use of a computer at home is discouraged.

- Technology is introduced at the high school level.[91]

Pierre Laurent, Waldorf Board President:

"How do you make children who are creative? How do you make children who are compassionate? All of that doesn't go through the screen. Computers don't encourage emotional connection." [92]

Canterbury Christian School (CCS)

- School philosophy: students learn in three stages (the grammar stage, the logic stage, and the rhetoric stage).
- Laptops, tablets, and cell phones are not allowed in the classroom.
- K-6 grade students are in the grammar stage; therefore, they need to focus on reading, writing, and arithmetic.
- Sixth graders and above are introduced to typing and researching online.

Steve Macias, Headmaster of CCS:

"Every major digital electronic tech company is represented in our parents here. The thing that they work every day promoting and selling, they don't want their children to touch."[93] Macias is focused on ensuring they are competent readers, and not so interested in teaching students the latest programs. He points out the programs will probably change ten times over by the time they complete college.

Something to Note:

In July 2018, France legally banned smartphones and other kinds of internet devices such as tablets in the school room for children ages 3–15.[94]

Conclusion

Chris Anderson, founder of Wired and CEO of 3D Robotics and the father of five children, may have said it best:

> "We thought we could control it. And this is beyond our power to control. This is going straight to the pleasure centers of the developing brain. This is beyond our capability as regular parents to understand."[95]

The same was true for me, I thought I could control it. My daughter and I had ongoing conversations regarding the dangers of social media and the internet until her eyes rolled back in her head. I set in motion random spot checks and time limitations. Finally, good old-fashioned trust was the crown jewel of my control plan. My motto was, "You have my trust until you prove otherwise." Admittedly, it was a colossal failure.

I was easily outrun and outflanked by my much younger, tech-savvy daughter. Intuitively, she understood her way around the internet and had advanced mastery of most tech devices—something I was sadly lacking.

While I was leading from behind, she was leaving no trace behind.

Moreover, I was void of critical information and lacking in crucial knowledge pertaining to the development of social media platforms. I was unaware and ignorant of the addictive component purposely built into online networks. Astoundingly, the tech industry widely acknowledges the unapologetic use and direct intention of capitalizing on addictive models integrated into social platforms in order to gain and hold consumer attention and loyalty.

The pioneers of big tech companies also like to do things differently when it comes to the education of their children. Unsurprisingly, many Silicon Valley parents choose to educate their children in private schools. I say, good for them. However, I was stunned to learn their schools of choice are those with the absence of technology in the classroom. Furthermore, the use of home computers is heavily discouraged by the school.

WHAT?

Wait a minute, are these not the same people who created, encouraged, promoted, and provided computers in the classroom for our children? Was this not the promise of advanced education? The hallmark of a nationally recognized blue-ribbon school? The wave of the future? This is the big little secret the rest of us were not let in on.

I find this outrageous considering the overwhelming commitment of the tech industry to transform our educational system with smart boards and computers.

Cofounder of HashCut and former Google employee,

Vijay Koduri, made the following observation regarding technology in schools:

> "The tech companies do know that the sooner you get kids, adolescents or teenagers used to your platform, the easier it is to become a lifelong habit. It's no coincidence that Google has made a push into schools with Google Docs, Google Sheets, and the learning management system Google Classroom."[96]

Yes, a simple assessment of our children's love affair with tech would certainly confirm his statement.

Nineteen

Internet Pornography and Sex Addiction

Imagine this: At ages eight and nine, I calmly had the appropriate conversations regarding where babies came from with my daughter. Once the basic mechanics had been covered, I looked forward to teaching her the more mysterious part of human relationships. Next would be the nuances of dealing with love, emotions, and morals as it relates to sex. Ideally, this would occur as she approached age ten-plus and started to notice boys. Sadly, before I had the chance to fill in the gray space, the internet would rip through my home like a category five hurricane that left nothing behind.

The infinite power of the World Wide Web had begun to dawn on me. The exposure my daughter experienced had affected and changed her. In hindsight, I began to connect her youthful impulsivity and internet pursuits as the core of numerous accelerated behaviors. It would take years to recover the missing pieces. Some of which would never be known to me. I was dealing with an unknown entity cloaked in shadows and anonymity. Clearly, my daughter had been entangled in the web.

Like many parents, I did my due diligence regarding technology in our home. Like a broken record, I continued the dialogues concerning the hidden dangers of the internet and the importance of staying vigilant. Upon the discovery my ominous words had not been heeded, I was exasperated. Soon after, I was angry, mostly at her . . . she had been warned numerous times. I held her accountable, insisting she was responsible for her choices. I held my parenting reins tight until gradually I came to realize she was truly the victim. A victim of society, a victim of her own curiosity, and most notably a victim of technology.

The following is a letter I wrote to my daughter when she was fifteen. By this time, she had completed a wilderness program and was in her second therapeutic boarding school.

Dear Daughter,

I have been thinking a lot about you and the path you have traveled for the last three years.

I want you to know you are not to blame for the things that have happened to you.

Please hear me:

At ten years old, you could not have known what exists on the dark side of life. Your curiosity was not wrong. Unfortunately, access to technology and a simple touch of a button exposed you to things no little girl should ever see or know. In an instant you were robbed of your innocence and I was robbed of you. You could not have known what you were about to see. You had no ability to predict what would happen.

I can't even begin to imagine or know what that moment was like for you. I know what it was like for me . . . it was shocking, gut wrenching, horrifying, traumatizing, heartbreaking, and sad. How could you even process or understand what you were seeing?

How could you understand the things you were feeling? I can't imagine the storm inside your head.

Please know:

What happened to you was not natural. You were not expected to handle this on your own. I hope you know that. You still are not expected to handle this on your own. I am so very sorry I was not there at that moment for you. It was and is my job to protect you.

I wish I could undo this for you. I wish you could unsee what you saw. But sadly, it is not possible. We have to treat the trauma you experienced; we have to heal the wound. We can't push it away because if we do, it will continue to manifest itself in your life. You already know this based on your behavior online over break. You will never escape it unless and until you confront it. It is the monster in the room.

Finally, let me apologize for the complicated world you live in. It is a lot for a young person to manage. I wish you could be free to figure yourself out without unforgiving consequences.

Love,

Mom

An Addictive Habit

"Just as a heroin addict chases a substance-induced high, sex addicts are binging on chemicals—in this case, their own hormones."[97] —*Alexandra Katehakis*

Pornography addiction: a strong and harmful need to regularly engage with erotic materials in an effort to create adequate and intense natural physical reaction.

How Does It Happen?

- **Dopamine** - the basis for addiction. Repeated interactions with porn release this chemical and encourage more behavior in order to repeat the experience. It is responsible for creating cravings.

- **Tolerance** - desensitization to porn leads to multiple viewings of intense pornography, ultimately leading to greater volume. The brain is not meant to handle high immediate and consistent levels of dopamine.
- **Addiction** - as the desire to watch pornography is indulged, the tolerance continues to increase and eventually a block builds between the reward center and the judgment center in the brain. Self-control is lost. Addiction occurs.[98]

So What's the Big Deal?

- **Potential for addiction** - the desire to continually assess pornographic material and the inability to stop.
- **Expansion of pornographic boundaries** - upon repeated exposure, there is possible desire to explore outside the original comfort zone.
- **Turning pornographic images into reality** - the next step would be a desire to act out pornographic scenarios in real life.
- **Porn misrepresents reality** - it does not reflect how real people look, act, and behave in intimate relationships. Resulting in unrealistic and unhealthy expectations.[99]
- **Interference with relationships** - creates preconceived ideas of what is expected sexually in an intimate relationship. Impacts the ability to build and maintain healthy relationships.

- **Creates lifelong struggle** - sexual addiction can set up a lifelong struggle in which the youth's focus, biological reward system, and behavior are interwoven with themes of sexual pleasure.
- **Exposure to further addiction** - medical literature supports the premise that a young person with one addiction is likely to have another.[100]
- **At risk legally for sex offending** - simply put, viewing sexual content of those underage or while underage can be legally problematic.[101]

Connecting the Dots

- Internet access is readily available and provides no boundaries.
- Pornography on the internet is a dangerous playground. Self-control goes to the wayside with the ability to be anonymous behind screen names, etc.
- Small mobile devices make pornography available anywhere and at any time.
- A 2015 meta-analysis of 22 studies from seven countries found that internationally the consumption of pornography was significantly associated with increases in sexual aggression, both verbally and physically among males and females alike.[102]
- A survey found that 53% of boys and 39% girls believe that pornography is a realistic depiction of sex. (NSPCC 2016).[103]
- Among adolescents age 12–16, pornography addiction impairs recent verbal memory (2019).[104]

- Teen brains are still growing at a rapid rate and are malleable, therefore making the effects of pornography more extreme and detrimental.
- "Addiction is an extension of reward-based learning that can physically alter the brain and affect behavior."[105]

Dr. Sharon Cooper, forensic pediatrician and faculty member at UNC school of medicine states that, "Imagery definitely affects children."[106] According to Dr. Cooper, pornography normalizes sexual harm by portraying a lack of emotional relationship between consensual partners, unprotected sexual contact, and in some instances of violence and rape.

She argues further, "Youth are more vulnerable to pornographic images because of mirror neurons in the brain, which convince people they are actually experiencing what they see. Mirror neurons play an important role in how children learn. Children learn in part by observing and imitating behaviors."[107]

Chemical Connection: It's Complicated

- Viewing pornography releases the hormone dopamine in your brain. This is what creates the craving.
- At the same time oxytocin and vasopressin, two other hormones are also released. Their job is to lay down neural pathways of memory and link them with any pleasurable sensations we feel.

- The brain also releases endorphins. These create the feeling of being high and euphoric.
- Finally, there is a feeling of calm and relaxation produced by serotonin.[108]

Scientific studies have recently shown this type of addiction is nearly identical to alcohol or heroin addiction. They have the following traits in common:

- Increased tolerance over time.
- Loss of control and impulsive behavior.
- Painful physical and psychological withdrawal.
- Abnormal social behavior.[109]

Conclusion

We are losing our youth, literally and figuratively. We have a real problem with pornography and sex trafficking, not to mention bullying, addiction, and suicide. Regrettably, this is nothing new in the history of mankind.

What is new?

The integration and use of technology in our everyday lives. A predator's ability to strategically use a twenty-first-century device wielded as a weapon to target an unsuspecting victim.

What is unknown?

The widespread and deep-reaching effect internet pornography has on our youth.

What is different?

The lack of boundaries in how, when, and where children have opportunities to discover sex through the viewing of internet pornography.

We as parents have willingly bankrolled our children's desire for various forms of technology starting at a young age with electronic "learn while you play" toys. We have handed them Game Boys, Jr. Smartwatches, tablets, and iPads loaded up with apps, games, and movies. We have eagerly partnered with the educational system which continues to support our parental expectations through the use of smart boards, online requirements, and most recently virtual school. Unwittingly, we have set the wheels in motion for dependency and potential addiction to these devices, and with that, the predators lay in wait. Essentially, we have provided them with endless opportunities to interface with our children.

Kids, curious or otherwise, have been provided a powerful platform capable of producing an answer for any question they can think to ask, whether it is innocent or not. With an over-sexualized culture, eventual missteps are inevitable.

I am convinced exposure to pornography of any type at an early age is traumatic and impactful upon the brain and the essential nature of a human (life). The psyche of an individual becomes transformed into something it was not intended to be. A young person does not have the cognitive ability to process and assimilate this type of visual content. For that fact, I am not sure a healthy adult does either.

It is not as simple as a child accidentally being exposed to internet pornography through search engines, clickbait, or suggestions from YouTube. The process is complex, triggered by visual content creating a chain reaction of powerful chemicals firing in the brain, eventually leading to tolerance and a need to repeat the cycle. Perhaps more important are the mirror neurons that are simultaneously hard at work in a young person's brain. Children learn by observing and imitating.

There is a famous quote by Dr. Asa Don Brown: "Children are sponges, soaking up every verbal and non-verbal interaction." With her words in mind, the internet takes on a more concerning and disturbing meaning when we are talking about pornography. Internet porn is an intense visual with no explanation. This begs the question: What happens to a child's brain when powerful pornographic images have been experienced and a mental imprint is left behind?

The physical barrier between the adult bookstore down the street and children no longer exists. The gatekeeper has disappeared, leaving the internet a modern-day conduit for adult bookstores, affording the consumer a different level of access and privacy. With the convenience of a mobile device, participation can occur anytime and anywhere.

Ideally, the introduction to sex and sexual behavior for children is a gradual process guided by their parents. As a young mother, I remember being advised to address questions as they were asked. Most parents start simplistically with a basic explanation regarding the birds and the bees, eventually tackling the more delicate details associated with intimate relationships. The slow infusion of information allowed the adolescent time to process the data into knowledge. Even if a youngster gained sexual information from another outside source, it was still limited and subject to scrutiny.

Internet porn has robbed parents of the ability to do their job and teach their children about sex and intimate relationships through family and religious values. The natural boundaries have been destroyed.

Twenty

Online Predators

Very early on, my daughter found it difficult to form friendships with other children. She quickly established a pattern of making friends, and soon after would sabotage the fragile relationship based on a variety of reasons. Rinse and repeat. It was heartbreaking to watch.

I meticulously analyzed the tenacious personality of my daughter in an attempt to unravel the mystery surrounding her inability to connect. I concocted endless ways to teach her the hidden truths of friendship. Together we read books on the subject matter and role-played various scenarios. I even revealed my personal disappointments and shortcomings encompassing my own lost friendships.

Unaffected, she remained oblivious to the feelings of others, and as a result often demonstrated a glaring lack of empathy. An invisible barrier remained between her and the ability to experience an authentic connection.

The groundwork had been laid and somewhere between the social ups and downs of 4th and 6th grade, my daughter discovered new friends on the internet. It was a secret place in which to dwell and not only gain attention, but also acceptance.

My child stood little chance considering the skill set with which internet predators hunt their victims. Faceless deviants roam a virtual playground on which they pursue their naive and inexperienced prey with competence.

So, what happens when you take a ten-year-old whose frontal cortex is developing and add images of strong sexual content with no boundaries?

It is simple, the innocence of a child is destroyed. The sweet mystery of a young girl's first relationship is shattered. A heartbroken parent is left to pick up the pieces.

Where Predators Roam

"The United States is the number one consumer of sex worldwide. So, we are driving the demand as a society."[110] —*Geoff Rogers, Cofounder of the US Institute Against Human Trafficking*

- The US is one of the top three nations of origin for victims of human trafficking (2018).[111]
- In 2020 the CyberTipline received more than 21.7 million reports regarding sexual abuse images and online enticement, including "sextortion."[112]
- Registered sex offenders have the constitutional right to use social media platforms, Supreme

Court (June 19, 2017).[113]

- An offender (or anyone else) can legally take photos off of Facebook and post them elsewhere.

How Predators Have Infiltrated Social Media Apps

- YouTube (85% of teens ages 13–17 use) - Video-sharing platform that allows anyone to upload, view, or comment on content. Predators use the comment section for time-stamping videos and making comments.

- Snapchat (69% of teens ages 13–17 use) - A photo "snap" can be taken and sent to a recipient to be viewed for a specified amount of time. This creates a false sense of security, as the user thinks the snap has disappeared. The content of the snap gets stored in a database. Predators have infiltrated the database and used compromising photos to extort victims for sexually explicit photos.

- Instagram (72% of teens ages 13–17 use) - This platform has over 1 billion users worldwide. It is used for sharing photos, videos, and interacting with family, friends, bloggers, and celebs. A feature on Instagram has the ability to look up or follow hashtags. This allows the user to follow a favorite subject. Predators have used #dropboxlinks (against Instagram's terms) among other hashtags to locate and share files containing porn. Predators also look

up hashtags such as #babybathtime or #dia-
perchange and steal photos for trading.[114]

- WhatsApp (owned by Facebook) - Allows 1.5 billion users to call, message, and video chat people all over the world. Users can send documents, PDFs, and spreadsheets. All that is needed is a device with internet connection. The chat function allows up to 256 people to chat at once, making it popular. Due to the end-to-end encryption security system used by WhatsApp, predators are known to move potential victims over (from the initial point of contact) to continue the grooming process in a more secure location.[115]

YouTube and Kik Special Mention

Both of these Social Media Platforms have a tremendous child predator issue:

- **YouTube** - How it works: Non-pornographic videos can be commented on and time-stamped (specific scenes) that sexualize the child in the video. These videos can be shared privately between users. The platform has 450 hours of content uploaded every minute and billions of users monthly. According to Matt Watson, a former YouTube creator, "YouTube's recommended algorithm facilitates pedophiles' ability to connect with each other, trade contact info, and link to actual child pornography in the comments."[116] YouTube had another event in 2017 (known as Elsagate) in which disturbing, sexualized kids' content was being recommended to kids.[117] Their algorithm has been widely criticized due to the limited number of clicks it takes to arrive at inappropriate content.

- **Kik** - It uses a smartphone's data plan or Wi-Fi to transmit and receive messages, photos, videos, sketches, mobile web pages, and other content after users register a username. It is instant messaging with anonymity. Registration does not require a phone number. Kik does not track content. You can access public chats to talk about any interest you have by using the search function. Predators can be members of an unlimited number of groups dedicated to trading child abuse material, pornographic images, and videos of minors. Kik has over 300 million users (US and Europe).[118] As documented by an officer in court, "Kik Messenger is frequently used by individuals to trade child pornography because it is free, simple to set up, easily accessible, potentially anonymous and allows users to share digital data privately."[119] Popular with kids because parents can't automatically view their kid's chats remotely. They must have a password and view chats on the same device.

Predators Will . . .

- scour social media sites and create a similar teen profile.
- compile information on kids by following their social media platforms.[120]
- ask to join their "clan" or chat group in online gaming.[121]
- clone another person on Facebook and then ask for a friend request.
- hang out in teen chat rooms.
- affirm feelings and choices of teens.[122]

Red Flags to Recognize Online Predators

- Want to have conversations in private.
- Ask a lot of questions and ask for personal information.
- Already know things about you and stalk you, your family, and friends online.
- Try to make you feel special and ALWAYS agree with you.
- Try to turn you against other people—they will tell you your family and friends don't understand you.
- Ask for pictures or ask to video chat.
- Make uncomfortable comments and ask you to lie.
- Pressure you to meet in person.
- Threaten you and make you think what they are doing is normal.[123]

How Predators Can Physically Locate You

- They use software that can extract GPS coordinates from pictures and posts.
- Much of the information uploaded to social media is geotagged and is easy for a predator to decipher.

What Is Geotagged?

Involves tagging a geographic location to a social media platform or something you post online. This provides your friends and followers a glimpse into where you are and what you're doing. For example, you can share the restaurant where you are dining. Most social networks have geotagging features built in (web version and mobile apps). You can geotag on Facebook, Twitter, Instagram, and Snapchat.

Predators and Teens: Reality Check (Based on the FBI's recent takedown of an international child porn ring)

- The men **masqueraded as teenage boys** using fake profiles and stolen pictures. They trolled popular teen social media sites (primarily MyLOL). They would comment on an older post (to gain attention and stand out) from others commenting on newer posts.
- Members had **assigned roles**: Hunters, Talkers, Loopers.
- **Hunters** - sought out girls on social media sites

who were lonely, vulnerable or bored. The end game was to lure them to chat rooms (where no one would police their activities).

- **Talkers** - once in the chatroom, the talkers took over, spending time building rapport and trust through attention and compliments. The ultimate goal was to convince girls to undress and engage in sexual activity. A variety of **manipulative techniques** were used to get the girls to undress and sexually perform on camera. Namely dares, polls, and competitions. They challenged the minors with a dare to engage in simple things such as removing clothing. The group would conduct polls about which girls were pretty or cute and had nice eyes. The polls graduated into votes about whether the victim should remove items of clothing or engage in other sexual activity. The group would sometimes pit the girls in competitions for points. Points were gained by taking off the most clothing and/or engaging in sexual activities. The girls could go from "level one" to "level two" by gaining points.

- **Loopers** - Their job was to entice the girls into making sexual videos "by playing previously recorded videos of boys performing sex acts."

- "The group kept close track on the girls, including their names, links to social media accounts and chat rooms that they visited."

- These female victims ranged in age from 8–17.[124]

Sextortion: Threats to Expose Sexual Images

- **Type one**: A romantic or sexual relationship where an aggrieved partner threatens the exposure of images to force a reconciliation or as revenge.
- **Type two**: When a perpetrator meets a target online and uses a sexual image to demand more sexual images—45% of the time, perpetrators carry out their threats.[125]

A Sextortion Ring in Action

- **First Step** - A teen meets an "online friend" on a monitored, mainstream social media platform and begins a conversation. A specialist poses as a peer and identifies a target.
- **Second Step** - once the relationship is started, the kid is moved to a second, less monitored sight (Google Hangout, WhatsApp, Kik). Lack of monitoring and privacy is key. They now have a new handler who is skilled at building the relationship and obtaining sexual pics and videos.
- **Third Step** - after the kid has sent the pics, they are handed off again to another specialist. This is when the pictures or videos are used to blackmail the kid for more product. The specialist may demand more pics in return for not exposing them on social media, otherwise known as sextortion.[126]

Additional Predator Playgrounds: Facebook, Twitter, Tumblr, TikTok, Flickr, Meetup, Tinder, Myspace, Kik, Tango, Nitefort, Minecraft, Clash of Clans, Call of Duty, Grand Theft Auto, among others.

Conclusion

These are not the days of yesterday.

Most of us were taught as kids about "stranger danger." The scenario featured the creep on the street ready to physically lure you into his beat-up windowless van with a sad story of his lost puppy. In sharp contrast, today we teach our children about internet dangers involving a different type of faceless predator with an unknown physical location working to hook them into an online friendship.

The present-day predator is one who no longer works in the streets, on the playground, or even in your front yard. They work from a computer, targeting your child any time of the day or night, wherever they may happen to be. This includes the perceived safety of a bedroom, where your child lays their head down to go to sleep while texting their friends goodnight. It includes the carpool line, where your child sits in the backseat with their iPad or mobile device. It includes the restaurant where your child passively entertains themselves while the adults dine. In other words, it is anytime and anywhere your child has technology in their hands.

It is not enough to teach kids the basics of internet safety. It is not enough to apply parental controls to their technology and wait for the text alert. It is far more complicated than that. Predators use complex and sophisticated systems in order to gain access to children. They use other children to connect with your children, going so far as to clone another young person's profile on Facebook and then ask for a friend request. An internet predator can easily stalk your child using online profiles to identify the places your child frequents such as coffee shops, book stores, or sporting events. It is not difficult for the predator to take the next step and show up in the same places as your child. Not only will he show up, but he will also come armed with personal information that makes him appear familiar to your child . . . all gained from social media platforms.

In many cases, our children do not go looking for it. The deviant individuals engaging in sexploitation will come looking for them. They are specialists in emotional manipulation. They will find your child on their cell phone, tablet, computer, and gaming system. Make no mistake, they will find them.

Consider the following: Your child is participating in a team sports event and while you are the proud parent, you do not upload video or photos to YouTube or Facebook; however, the parent standing next to you does. "It is just sports," you say. True, but it is more than that. It is the ability for anyone to edit and manipulate an image of a young gymnast, cheerleader, or volleyball player in booty shorts. All done without our knowledge or consent.

Dig deeper and evaluate the idea that chat rooms, apps, gaming, and social media platforms make their followers and users one big community of shared ideas. But who is in the community? When you use a dating app, car share app, or babysitting app, who is the person on the other side? Most of us cannot answer that question and neither can our children.

It is very challenging, if not close to impossible, to live in a tech-free world. This became apparent to me when I provided my daughter with a temporary flip phone while traveling from boarding school to home. Once she cleared airport security, she would be unescorted to her gate and I was concerned with her inability to communicate with me or the school. What if she missed the flight or was delayed? How would she contact me? One does not exactly find public telephones in airports anymore. After purchasing the most basic stripped-down "burner phone" manufactured, I was shocked to learn it had internet capability. In addition, I was further annoyed to discover the phone's ability to download limited proprietary apps, not to mention a camera feature. I could scratch out the lens on the camera (which I did), but I could not block the internet. I contacted the manufacturer, and asked for directions on how to block access to the internet, which ultimately turned out to be impossible not to mention a waste of my time. To the best of my knowledge, the basic flip phones of the past no longer exist.

Another similar situation popped up while my daughter was in boarding school. She asked for a Game Boy as a birthday gift; something you might expect a much younger kid to request. It had been many years since I had purchased this handheld tech game. The early generations (originally produced in 1989) had cartridges that were inserted into the device in order to play and did not require internet connection. The biggest concern was keeping up with all of the cartridges. *No harm, no foul,* I thought to myself as I worked to fill her request. I soon discovered they did not make any version of this game without internet capability. In any other circumstance, downloading games via the internet would be a welcomed convenience; however, from my vantage point, it was an avenue providing an open door to other possibilities and potentially trouble.

Twenty-One

North Carolina and Texas
The Internet, Sexting, and the Law

My dad had a saying when I was growing up, "I can't make you do anything, but I can make you wish to hell you had." That left an indelible impression on me and obviously I never forgot it. To a large degree, it was what kept me in line.

Today, there is still great wisdom in his words. However, the forces of an untamed internet are stronger than they have ever been, and that makes it a game changer when it comes to how we parent.

The law can certainly make you wish to hell you had, or rather had not.

When I placed a smartphone in my daughter's hands at the age of ten, I essentially handed her Pandora's box. Even worse, I allowed her to operate it behind a closed door. She was trustworthy, but the outside world was not. I knew this, but even as an experienced adult, I did not fully understand how quickly things could get out of hand.

Foolish choices and careless failure to protect private information has resulted more than once in disastrous outcomes personally and legally for multitudes of individuals. Many times, I have wondered to myself, *What were they thinking?* With further reflection, I am reminded that being gullible is not age discriminant. Sadly, there are plenty of well-informed adults who have become casualties of social media missteps.

If that's the case, then how in the world could I expect my young daughter to understand how easy it is to place herself in irreversible media jeopardy? It simply is not a reasonable expectation.

Internet crimes are uncharted territory for most parents. It is difficult to conceptualize how a young person and their families could get caught in a legal web through actions perceived as harmless. It is more possible than you might imagine.

Legal Complexities and Potential Consequences

"People pay for what they do, and still more, for what they allow themselves to become. And they pay for it simply: by the lives they lead." —*Edith Wharton*

North Carolina WARNING: NC currently does not have laws that address sexting behavior of minors. Anyone engaging in sexting behavior (minors included) can be charged and convicted under child pornography laws, which is a felony.[127]

Simply Stated: A minor who is in possession of their own sexually explicit photos is still subject to child pornography laws.

Consequences of a Child Pornography Conviction

- A juvenile will be tried as an adult in superior court.
- Registered as a federal sex offender, resulting in mandated living restrictions, restriction to licensing boards, including education and employment limitations.[128]
- Incarceration - 5 years or more with fines of $5,000 or more.
- Probation - 12 months under legal supervision.[129]

Texas WARNING: "Activity on the internet falls under the jurisdiction of both state and federal laws. Breaking the law online can lead to similar criminal penalties as breaking the law in person."[130]

The majority of sex crimes have to do with perpetrating sexual activity against a person who does not consent to the activity or who cannot consent to the activity. (By law, a minor cannot consent simply due to the fact that they are a minor.) For this reason, many internet sex crimes occur when an adult attempts to engage in illegal activity involving minors and children.[131]

Sexting in Texas

Teens in Texas are punished under the state law "against electronically transmitting sexual depictions of children."[132]

Simply Stated: It is illegal for one minor to electronically send an image of someone younger than 18 years old to another minor that includes images of the sender, recipient, or another underage person.

Texas teen defense: "Minors have a defense to prosecution when the images are solely of the sender or recipient, were sent within a dating relationship, and both parties are not more than two years apart in age."[133]

Who Suffers the Consequences?

- Teens can be charged.
- People who received and shared the photo can be charged.
- Parents or guardians of teens can be charged (under Texas child enticement or endangerment laws for allowing the teens involvement in illegal sexual activities).

Possible Penalties for a Juvenile

- Warning.
- Fine.
- Community service or counseling.
- Probation - a teen must comply with a set of orders as defined by the court for a period of time.
- Detention - the court can order teens into detention centers, home confinement, group homes, or alternate placement.

Possible Penalties for Adult Sexting with a Minor

- Incarceration - potential prison sentence of 20 years.
- Fines - up to $10,000.
- Probation - 12 months, but typically more.
- Sex offender registry - person must register with the state. Law enforcement track where you live and must be notified every time you move. These usually last for a period of 10 years.

Bottom Line:

Laws in this area are generally nonexistent or rapidly evolving and can differ greatly by jurisdiction.

Conclusion

This is what I now know:

The moment impulsivity takes hold in the world of sexting, there is little to stop it from becoming the same moment life is breathed into a monster that cannot be shackled. At the same time, the power to control one's image and reputation has been forfeited and left behind on the internet highway. There is no way to control what happens to an image once it has been posted privately or otherwise. Anyone can copy, share, or manipulate an image without the knowledge or consent of the individual. In some states, if the image is pornographic in nature, both the sender and receiver can face felony charges.

Most kids have a false sense of privacy when engaged on the internet behind a closed door. They cannot see the world of virtual strangers they have invited into the room because they are physically alone and feel secure. A computer screen blurs the boundaries of safety and reality, and as a result misrepresents the connection between actions and potential consequences of those actions.

Teenagers can also be naive and trusting of the unspoken boundaries and expectations of an intimate relationship or friendship, forgetting not everybody plays by the same rules. Online betrayal can be devastating.

The current attitude among teenagers toward sexting is generally casual, and often it is expected or coerced in relationships; many become participants actively or passively. It is so prevalent that most teens do not consider it to be a big deal. Unfortunately, the ability to conceptualize the full realm of possible outcomes is more than their developmental age allows for. Consequently, few teenagers understand the full legal ramifications of sexting.

Gaining a basic education regarding the laws in my state left me shocked and with renewed respect toward the forces of the modern Wild West. The power of the internet to disrupt lives and the ability of youth to comprehend the capacity of that power is a disproportionate match of enormous measure. There are countless ways for any child to unknowingly place themselves, as well as their family, in legal peril.

Twenty-Two

Reality Check with Private Investigators and Law Enforcement

One of the more naive, not to mention jarring, comments my young daughter made to me centered around what she would do in the event of being confronted by a predator.

She insisted she had a plan. The plan involved simply not doing anything she did not want to do; she could refuse and leave. She was confident she could get away because she was smart, fast, and strong. More importantly, she would not allow herself to get in that situation in the first place; noting she would give them false information and never meet in person. She believed using the computer from the safety of her bedroom created a natural barrier between her and the bad guys. She was convinced she could play them and they could not get to her.

With nervous tension creeping up the back of my neck, I countered by vividly painting a horrific picture of someone overpowering her and jabbing a needle in her neck, immediately rendering her helpless. Unimpressed, she was certain her internet friends were harmless and anything but predators, making our conversation an instant non-issue.

She did not know the depth of possibilities when in the grip of a child predator; in truth, I did not know either. With that in mind, I sought to find out.

Facts, Candor, and the Bottom Line

"I used to sell cocaine, but then I figured out you can only sell a gram of cocaine once, but I can sell a woman over and over again." —*Confession of a drug trafficker to an undercover detective*

Human trafficking: an individual being deceived or coerced into prostitution, forced labor, or domestic servitude.

Rania Mankarious, Executive director of Crime Stoppers of Houston, explains how a trafficker grooms a child by befriending them on social media or in person:

> "They start introducing them to something the child would not normally do. This phase usually involves drugs, alcohol or pornography. Then they use that to start to create some sort of division between parents and then friends. Then

they start isolating the child from the family. Eventually they are usually drugged, tattooed or branded. Photos are taken of them, they are sold online, and they are exploited."[134]

Mankarious warns traffickers look like everybody else and often use other children to recruit.[135]

Allen Cardoza, a licensed private investigator with over thirty years' experience, specializes in locating, and returning runaway teens and rescuing abducted children. He shares the following insights: "One heinous crime against children is getting them to send sexually compromising pictures to the predator who in turn sells to pornographic websites for money, exposing kids to all types of sick individuals. It is an ugly world most people don't know too much about and probably don't want to." [136]

Invisible Handcuffs

Cardoza stated, "In many cases, exploited young people are so ashamed of what has happened, they are afraid to even try to go home or tell their parents. How do you tell your parents, 'I was so stupid and believed them. I went with them and then realized they didn't like or love me after they locked me in a room and did terrible things to me.'"

Who Is Most Vulnerable?

- Children seeking friends through social media.
- Kids disenchanted with their families.
- Runaways needing shelter.

The Predator's Promise

- Predators promise to treat them better than others do.
- Predators promise material items others cannot provide.
- Predators promise to provide food and shelter.
- Predators promise a level of freedom young people do not believe they have at home.

Human traffickers will shelter a runaway and then ask them to pay for their upkeep through sex for a fee.

Cardoza's Advice to Parents

- **Early communication.** Talk to your kids at a young age. Let them know how much you love them and that you will always be there for them without judgment, no matter what.
- **Be present.** You must be in the moment with your kids. They need your time. This can be a challenge when you are working hard and have an abundance of responsibilities. The quality time you spend with them is of more value than the extra items purchased by working overtime.

- **Know their friends.** Parents often have incomplete information and sometimes no information at all regarding friends. Have the full names, addresses, and phone numbers of your child's friends.

- **Parents need to parent.** Do not worry about whether your kid likes you or is mad at you. Kids do not need a forty-five-year-old friend.

- **Be proactive.** Identify and address the issues your child is experiencing. If unaddressed, these are the kids who often end up on the streets and ultimately are not found until after they have been trafficked.

Special Note: Predators will coach children (especially young children) how to erase their history. Just because you find nothing when you check their computer, does not mean it is not happening.

An Interview with a Police Lieutenant in a Major Metropolitan City: Internet Crimes Against Children Task Force:[137]

Common types of internet crimes committed against children online:

- Solicitation of a minor.
- Possession or promotion of child pornography.
- Obscene display or distribution.
- Electronic transmission of certain visual material depicting a minor.

- Possession or promotion of lewd visual material depicting minors.

Common tools a sexual predator uses to attract a child on the internet:

- Applications.
- Video games.
- Chat rooms.

"Wherever you have children, you will also have child predators. Predators hang out in chat rooms, play games, and download applications used by children in hopes that they can meet, groom, and abuse them. One of the most common forms of this is seen in gaming applications. Predators play games popular with children (Roblox, Fortnite, etc.) and they befriend them in order to groom them."

How hard is it to track down and prosecute an internet sexual predator?

"This process is very detailed and lengthy. The reason for this is that technology is involved and it takes time to build a solid investigation regarding the use of the technology. Law enforcement officers need to be certain they have the right person, and once they have them identified, prosecution is fairly certain. Once a predator has been identified and an arrest warrant is issued, tracking them down and arresting them is not difficult. We have a very high success rate of apprehension once charges are filed."

Do you have a division specifically for internet crimes against kids?

"Yes, the Internet Crimes Against Children Unit is part of the Special Victims Division. There are sixty-one task forces in the nation with a total of three task forces in Texas."

Once a kid makes a connection with a sexual predator in person, what typically happens next?

"Sexual predators groom children prior to actually meeting with them in person. In the event that a child meets a sexual predator in person, they are almost always (I can't say always) victimized sexually by the predator. They have communicated for some time with these predators who have built a certain level of trust and friendship with these children. There is a high probability that sexual intercourse has already been discussed with these children prior to the first meeting and the willingness to go through with the intercourse has been established prior to meeting with the child."

When a kid gets caught in the sex trade, what is the likelihood of getting them back?

"While my division does not investigate child sex trade, there is some crossover with our investigations. I don't have statistics on the success of getting a child back from their trafficker; however, I would venture to say it all depends on the living/family relations of the child along with location and resources of the traffickers. If a child has a family in which no one is looking for them, the likelihood of them being recovered would decrease."

If a kid has been interfacing with a predator online, is there anything a parent can do to hold the predator legally accountable?

"Legally, a predator can be charged with Online Solicitation of a Minor if they have violated the elements of the offense. If a predator is interfacing with a child and there has been no sexual solicitation, then nothing can be done until they violate that criminal statute. In the event that a crime is committed, they can be charged and convicted. If they are charged, a criminal may also be sued civilly."

What advice would you give parents to protect their kids online? What is the most important thing you want parents to know?

"In order to protect your children online, you must know the following:

Who are they talking to?

- "Are these 'friends' your kid knows in person or just over the internet?"

- "Have they ever met these individuals before in person?"
- "Don't allow your children to ever be friends with someone they don't know in person."
- "Predators pretend to be children all the time to get information from children so they can meet them."

When are they online?

- "Know when your child is online. Do this by keeping the computer in a centralized location."
- "*Turn off the Wi-Fi* at night so that cellular service would be used to connect to the internet. This is an easy way to know if your child is online in the middle of the night when you think they are asleep."

Know what apps they are using.

- "Look at your child's apps and know what they are using."
- "Know who they are friends with on these apps."
- "*Monitor your child's photo library* for explicit images."
- "*Monitor your child's text messages* for explicit images and messages."

Watch out for Vault Apps (also known as hidden apps).

- "Certain applications will allow kids to hide images and messages."

- "These apps can often be disguised as a calculator or other application. If you kid has two calculators on their phone, one of them is fake."

What should you keep an eye out for?

"If your kid seems alarmed when you walk in the room and they are on their device, they are hiding something from you!"

Be involved and communicate with your kid.

- "If you don't speak to your child, the predators will."
- "Develop a relationship with your child and do not punish them, but educate them."
- "Children who are victims of sexual predators are victims! These people are very good about making someone believe them and it is not difficult for them to trick and lure your children."

Set rules for your children.

- "Expect them to follow the rules."
- "Don't allow the electronic device to be the babysitter."

What is the most obvious mistake(s) parents are making with their kids in regards to the internet?

"Deleting evidence is one of the biggest mistakes parents make.

If you find out your child is a victim, do not delete the images and messages. Your child will not be criminally charged when they are the victim. Parents often will delete the images or messages because they don't want their child to be in trouble with law enforcement. When they do that, they have gotten rid of precious evidence we need to make a case."

Don't treat your child like a criminal when you find out they are a victim.

"They have been groomed by a predator and they are a victim. Punishing them will make them withdraw from you and it will make it more difficult to get information from them. Remember, many of these predators have spent months grooming and building trust with your child. These kids feel like these predators are their friends and that the predator understands them. When a parent finds out that the child has been communicating with the predator and punishes them, that causes them to draw closer to the predator who seems to understand them."

Knowing each case is unique, can you outline a general scenario as to what happens in a typical internet crime?

"Once we receive the investigation, the first step for us is to *preserve the evidence.* This is done by contacting the internet service provider or company who operates the app to make sure the evidence is not deleted. We then work on *legal documents to identify the suspect.* Often this requires that we execute a search warrant on the residence of the suspect to search for the evidence. If a child has been victimized, they will also be *interviewed at a child advocacy center by a forensic interviewer.* If sexually assaulted by the suspect, there will also be a *sexual assault exam conducted* to determine if biological evidence exists.

If a suspect is identified and detained, they are then interviewed by investigators and criminal charges are filed. Often, their devices are examined by a digital forensics lab to recover items needed for court. This is all a very lengthy process due to the need for evidence recovery. These investigations take several months to work and can be delayed for various reasons."

Conclusion

"Don't treat your child like a criminal when you find out they are a victim," was sage advice from the police lieutenant and it resonated deeply with me. In some ways, I suppose I did treat my daughter like a criminal by locking her down, confiscating her technology, and ultimately sending her to live in the wilderness before continuing on to therapeutic boarding school. There is little doubt she lived with the recurring voice inside her head telling her she somehow deserved it and as a result that made her a bad person. She was not a bad person, but she had become tangled up with bad people and needed a way out.

To be sure, the devoted parent inside me struggled with the course of action to be taken, but in the end, I whole-heartedly believed I had no other choice if she was going to live to see another day.

When speaking to Private Investigator Allen Cardoza, I had several "aha" moments. There were many basic mistakes I made and did not even realize it.

In our conversation, I mentioned how astonished I was that my daughter, a mere ten years old at the time, was smart enough to erase her internet history. Cardoza quickly clued me in that more than likely, the predator instructed her how to do so; it was possible but not probable she thought to delete the history on her own volition. It never crossed my mind this might be the case.

My narrow and limited vision of a child being held captive by a predator involved drugs, chains, ropes, and a locked door leading to a windowless concrete room. I did not consider the invisible prison of shame. The experience of shame itself can be so powerfully paralyzing that it alone can hold a child captive emotionally and physically for a lifetime. A child who has been sexually exploited and trafficked may be unable to see themselves as anything other than what they were trafficked for. Cardoza stressed the importance of providing an opportunity for therapeutic healing and redirection.

In hindsight, another critical mistake I made was to erase the vast majority of evidence. Upon discovery, my instinct was to immediately rid myself and my daughter of the searing pain of such a visual reality, much like frantically brushing ants off of a child who just sat in an ant bed. The rapid-fire response was to strip her instantly of the harsh truth I had exposed. In addition, I was deeply protective of her and did not want anyone else to lay eyes on the sordid text messages or images I had seen and she had lived. At that moment, it did not occur to me I was disposing of potentially crucial evidence.

Finally, I was stricken with sheer panic upon the realization I was the parent who would not be able to fully provide a private investigator or law enforcement officer complete information regarding my child's friends. Yes, I had the school directory and was aware of her school friends, but these were not the ones she was talking to. I had failed to consistently comb her entire contact list and insist she identify them all.

There is an urgent and necessary need to re-establish a tangible definition regarding friendship in the modern age of social media. Not everyone is a friend; yet, on multiple social platforms we identify everyone as a friend. Our children do not differentiate between online and offline friendships. It is imperative we make the distinction of who is a real friend and who is not. A real friend is someone they know in person, not through the internet or through another friend on the internet.

Twenty-Three

Avoiding the Tech Trap

What can we do to keep from falling into the tech trap?

As we all know, progress moves at warped speed in the digital world. Our kids are often on to the newest tech discovery before we have figured out the last one. It is easy for parents to blink and miss. How I handled my kids' use of technology in 2010 and what I would do today are very different.

I certainly do not have all the answers, only conclusions from experience. I also have the benefit of hindsight. Having said that, there are six things I would definitely do differently.

1. **Delay technology**

2. **No tech EVER behind a closed door**

3. **Have all passwords and check up on them!**

4. **Educate yourself and your child**

5. **Be aware of the power of educational options**

6. **Create an agreement of accountability around technology**

1. Delay technology

I cannot even remember how old my daughter was when she received her first iPad, but I suspect she was around three years of age. It just sort of happened. We did not run out and purchase a brand new one; rather she inherited an older outdated version, handed down from a family member. An action I considered mindful and necessary in order to avoid a sense of entitlement toward the latest in digital devices.

Candidly, I did not want her on my devices; as a result, she was allowed her own. It was for my convenience and her entertainment. Age-appropriate movies, music, and educational games were easily downloaded, creating an efficient all-in-one entertainment source. You could bring it in the car, in the grocery store and even out to dinner. The iPad was the modern-day version of the television, small enough to slip down into your tote bag, making it a treasured resource of distraction for kids. The technology was a great assist in keeping my kid occupied while I was attending to other things.

I gave my daughter her first cell phone at age ten. I viewed it as a rite of passage. She was officially a pre-teen and becoming more independent. When at school, she would need a way to communicate with me and it proved mutually beneficial for me to let her know I was running late or plans had changed. In addition, my older children were in the family group text, and she should be too. There was also a certain comfort in knowing her exact location that put my mind at ease. I could fill pages with justifications for my actions.

I was so wrong. I had just fallen into the first part of the tech trap.

I believed I was hurting her by not letting her have these devices, when in fact I was hurting her because I did. Unknowingly, I had already begun to lay the groundwork for creating a potentially addictive desire for digital devices, not to mention a virtual substitute for real friendship.

She did not need these gadgets to be entertained. She did not need to run academic drills on educational apps in order to learn. In hindsight, I should have severely limited and delayed ALL tech as long as reasonably possible. Why?

The frontal cortex, where executive functioning occurs, is not fully developed until twenty-five years of age. This is the part of the brain where people learn to reason, control impulsivity, behavior and emotions. Clearly, we cannot delay tech until a person is twenty-five years old. But we can hold off specifically on smart phones until they are closer to fourteen and even as late as sixteen years of age; giving them more of an opportunity to make better decisions based on development and experience. Ten years old was regrettably too young.

2. No tech EVER behind a closed door

You would think this one is obvious. Not so much. Today's schools are built around personal computers and the convenience they bring. Homework and written assignments are managed on-line often through Google Docs. Students are frequently directed to the internet where they can access quizzes in preparation for exams. School grades and important parent communication are made easily accessible through online portals. It is easy for a student to justify a quiet private space behind a closed door in order to do homework uninterrupted.

Aside from an academic life online, most kids seek their personal entertainment through a variety of digital devices. Music, games, YouTube, and other forms of social media can be instantly accessed through a laptop computer, iPad, smartphone, and even to a lesser degree an Apple watch. This is the manner in which our children socialize and connect with the outside world. The retreat of a bedroom provides the perfect personal space in which to be digitally entertained. Furthermore, parents often welcome the breathing space tech distraction provides. Sounds reasonable.

I had just fallen into the second part of the tech trap.

The virtual strangers walked into my home, moved

stealthily past me, and climbed the stairs leading to my daughter's bedroom. It happened just that easily. In fact, they had been living in my home for over two years before I discovered them. They were there for her any time of the day or night. They did not have rules for her, but they did have expectations. They were masters of manipulation and pressure. I did not knowingly allow this scum into my home, but I did give them access. Quite simply, the possibilities associated with the internet were larger than I could wrap my mind around.

3. *Have all passwords and check up on them*

Yes, it does say in the parent manual: *Have all passwords.* It also says to check their accounts frequently.

Back in 2013, checking a device meant physically having the device in hand. It was necessary to methodically open each email, text, and social media platform and literally look around while at the same time hoping you were policing in the right area. Crucial to the process was knowing how to access the history, follow the cookies, and search the trash can. I understood two out of three techniques.

As you might imagine, this could be very time consuming. So, here was my reality: I had three kids at home moving in three different directions. The days and nights were jam packed and would often slip away before I was able to thoroughly check all their devices. I was inconsistent at best. In addition, my teenagers knew how to keep their internet interest hidden from prying parental eyes; frankly they were the ones I was focused on when more of my attention should have been on my youngest. As far as passwords are concerned, I did not do a great job keeping up with all of mine, much less three additional people. As my older kids were fast approaching the end of high school, I also began to question the point of such intense device oversight. Was Mommy going to check their devices while they were away at college? Of course not. I again could fill pages with justifications of why I fell short in this area.

I had just wandered into the third tech trap.

Truthfully, I found myself overwhelmed and intimidated attempting to keep current on social media sites, hidden apps, and clickbait in the form of cleverly disguised ads placed on popular websites. Admittedly, I did not understand how it all worked. Further complicating matters were the concepts of trust and privacy (which I wanted to afford my kids). Those privileges were in conflict with the necessary act of "parental stalking" on social media. To fully honor privacy in the world of social media is to play Russian Roulette with your child's well-being and future.

Currently there are numerous options for monitoring online activities (see list in chapter 28). That is good news, but I would not count entirely on it.

4. Educate yourself and your child

I did not have a complete grasp or appreciation for the powerful influence social media has on a large population of our society. I lacked the ability to fully comprehend the many ways a predator could infiltrate a child's innocent recreation on a popular app, as evidenced by my placing the scrutiny of my youngest child's internet pursuits on the back burner. The immersion of society into social connection and entertainment online was foreign to me, and I simply lacked mastery of it.

I didn't even know I was caught in the fourth tech trap.

Knowledge is power. My quest for information regarding the internet began as a reaction to the technological weeds my daughter had wandered off into. I randomly began to research, with several key ideas in mind for her education. My mission was her safety in an online world; specifically, where predators were concerned. The deeper I dug, the more disconcerted I became. As information emerged, I began to realize the internet demanded far more than basic safety tip awareness. It commanded my undivided attention and full respect for its more sinister capabilities. Equally important, technology necessitates a substantial commitment to ongoing education around a rapidly evolving industry. Left unchecked, a child will innocently roam the same digital playground as a predator. One misstep in this virtual field of landmines and it is game over.

Society has now turned out the first generation born into a world with the internet. They are presently young adults. Their experiences are unique and include everything from completing education virtually, using the internet and social media to make a living, to becoming anxiety-ridden, depressed individuals who feel disconnected. The deciding factor is often as simple as temperament and personality.

5. *Be aware of the power of educational options*

Honestly, it did not occur to me that I had legal rights or options where digital devices in the classroom are concerned. I made a general assumption: technology was required in education in order to advance in a digital world. Truth be told, I also valued the integration of computers and the internet, believing my kids would be better prepared adults for the working world. I still believe this, however, I now give credence to the importance of keeping a watchful eye on the use of technology in the classroom.

I was oblivious to the potential of the fifth tech trap.

Looking back, if I had more insight into the development of the child adolescent brain, and the effect of digital devices on the learning process, I may have done things differently. Many of the parents in Silicon Valley who work in the tech industry certainly did. Quite a few send their children to the Waldorf School, with no technology exposure until high school. The academic policy is based on brain research and the effects on a child's nerve network, eye tracking, and neurotransmitter levels. The school emphasizes education using real materials over electronic material. Peer interaction and play free of social media is part of the development of strong executive-function capabilities.

Aside from developmental concerns, there are many current legal issues around students and technology in the classroom. They include issues of student privacy and the collection of student data. There are controversies surrounding how students learn through use of real materials vs. electronic material. There are concerns around a school's ability to spy on a student through school-issued digital devices.

We are still in the middle of an educational experiment, and no doubt technological literacy is a critical skill in the twenty-first century. Some children assimilate and manage a digital world better than others. For some, it is an opportunity to create and escape into an alternate reality.

What I do know is my daughter lived in a tech-free environment from ages twelve to sixteen. As a result, she developed beautiful cursive handwriting and can spell correctly. She also has the ability to remember phone numbers, home addresses, and even my credit card number. Without electronic options, she often wrote engaging letters and enjoyed reading at night before going to bed. She avoided falling into social media mishaps, mostly because it was not available to her. I am not convinced these skills would have developed if she had a digital device in her hand.

The point? *Let the Buyer Beware.*

Parents should be aware and thoughtfully consider the use of digital devices in the education of their children.

6. Create an agreement of accountability around tech

I absolutely had numerous straightforward conversations concerning the dangers of the internet and social media with my children. My ideal philosophy for parenting was if you talk to your children, they will talk to you. If you listen to your children and offer nonjudgmental direction, they will listen to you. If you remain open and available, they will seek you out for guidance without fear. My more realistic philosophy was children should suffer the natural consequences of their actions. I will teach you, but you will take ownership. Our agreements were verbal and understood. Great theories, but not so effective when it came to digital media.

And with this philosophy, I was caught in the final tech trap.

I was deficient in creating strong boundaries around technology in my household. The policy of innocence until proven guilty did nothing to safeguard my daughter from unintentionally or intentionally stumbling into the internet vortex. Our verbal agreements required constant revision and fell short in a digital world that changes daily.

I am not a huge fan of contracts between parents and children. Having said that, contracts serve a purpose. They outline and define agreements in a written context. They serve as reminders to both parents and children as to what was agreed upon. I loathe the idea of spying, but if I had it to do again, I would unapologetically use technology to clone her digital devices. I would strongly consider using any other parental tool I had access to. In turn, I would put her on notice that I had done so. Being transparent says: these are the rules and subsequent consequences; it is not about tricking you and waiting for you to mess up. I will use all methods available to protect you because I love you. The expectation is your child remains responsible for their decisions and ownership thereof.

A Final Word on Technology

Tim Kendall, Former Executive for Facebook, Former President of Pinterest, as stated in *The Social Dilemma*:

> "It is easy to lose sight of the fact these tools have actually created some wonderful things in the world. I mean there were meaningful systemic changes happening around the world because of these platforms that were positive. I think we were naive about the flip side of the coin."

Tristan Harris, Former Design Ethicist at Google and Cofounder of Center for Humane Technology, as stated in *The Social Dilemma*:

> "A lot of what we are saying sounds like it's one-sided doom and gloom. Ruining the world and ruining kids. But no, it's

confusing (technology) because it's simultaneously utopia and dystopia all at once."[138]

Parents are not going to put the technological genie back into the bottle. It will be up to us to decide what we allow and how we allow technology in our lives.

PART THREE

The Resources

Twenty-Four

Balancing the Process

As a parent, I asked numerous questions, but not every question was the right one. For example, I knew my daughter would be living in the wilderness; it never occurred to me that a basic overnight, protective shelter, probably in the form of a pup tent, would not be provided. Instead, the gear issued for sleeping accommodations consisted of a ground tarp, a one-half-inch-thick pad, sleeping bag without a pillow, and a wire dome covered in mosquito netting large enough to place over the head (this was used to keep the bugs off while sleeping).

I further assumed some sort of cleverly designed portable outhouse would be positioned over the newly dug outdoor toilet, providing privacy and a makeshift seat. My mind would not take me to a place where my child would be squatting over a hole in the ground every time she needed to go to the bathroom. There was a vast disconnect between the images conjured up in my mind and the real experience of the wilderness. As a result, I did not think to ask some very basic questions.

I cannot say if having this additional information on the front end would have affected my decision to send my daughter to the wilderness. I would like to think not; however, it would have made the burden of the judgment call that much heavier.

In hindsight, my perspective has been altered. The lack of these basic items may appear to be cruel and un-civilized, however, it is exactly their absence that allows for the process of stripping an adolescent of any sense of entitlement, subsequently removing the distractions that get in the way of creating gratitude for untainted living and primitive survival. It is in the very heart of this space where the real work begins and healing follows.

There is a delicate balance in this process. There are no absolutes or guaranteed promises because the world is an imperfect place. What you can be assured of is the course of action remains constantly fluid while everyone involved rises up to meet the needs of your child. The majority of professionals are dedicated and prepared to commit their vast experience and knowledge to healing adolescents with hope for a new beginning.

Twenty-Five

Professional Resources

Jane Samuel

Jane, a Certified Parent Coach, has spent her forty-year career working with youth (ages 8–25) and families, in both public school and therapeutic settings serving as an Admissions Director, Program Director, and Executive Director. Jane has led family wilderness expeditions with young adults and their parents, in addition to creating and facilitating multiple parent workshops targeting varying parental age groups. Jane holds a Master's degree.

Ms. Samuel recommends the following professional resources:

National Association of Therapeutic Schools and Programs
www.NATSAP.org

NATSAP is a national resource for professionals and parents who are looking for treatment options for young people. Member schools must meet current standards of evidence-based services, meet state and national requirements, and agree to ethical principles as outlined by the organization.

Independent Educational Consultants Association
www.IECAonline.com

IECA members are skilled professionals who assist parents in finding the right placement for their child. Members have a wide variety of expertise and focus that include college, traditional boarding, and day schools or therapeutic settings.

Therapeutic Consulting Association
www.therapeuticconsulting.org

TCA is an organization of professionals focused on helping families find appropriate therapeutic placement for their child. The organization focuses on collaboration, training and education, outcome-based research, ethical standards, and ongoing review of best practices.

All Kinds of Therapy
www.allkindsoftherapy.com

An online resource helping families and professionals assess and review current programs that might be appropriate for teens.

Outdoor Behavioral Healthcare Council

www.obhcouncil.com

An organization of outdoor behavioral health programs that creates ethical and program standards for wilderness therapy programs serving young people.

Association of Mediation and Transport Services
www.amats.org

An organization of transport and mediation specialists that sets ethical and best practices standards for transporting youth.

Struggling Teens
www.strugglingteens.com

An online newsletter for schools, programs, professionals, and parents to be up-to-date on current trends and offerings. Parents often use this as a resource to find professional help for their child.

Books:

Glow Kids: How Screen Addiction Is Hijacking Our Kids and How to Break the Trance by Nicholas Kardaras, PhD

Screen Schooled: Two Veteran Teachers Expose How Technology Overuse Is Making Our Kids Dumber by Joe Clement and Matt Miles

I-Gen: Why Today's Super-Connected Kids Are Growing Up Less Rebellious, More Tolerant, Less Happy—and Completely Unpre-

pared for Adulthood by Jean M. Twenge, PhD

Documentaries:

The Social Dilemma

Twenty-Six

The Questions to Ask

Angie Fusco

Angie completed her Bachelor of Science in Education from the University of Tennessee at Chattanooga and a Master of Education from Middle Tennessee State University. She also received her teaching certification from Missouri Baptist University. She has enjoyed a variety of career interests and worked as a recreational therapist, outdoor therapeutic field staff and supervisor, program administrator, special projects manager, Director of Organizational Development for a leading adolescent mental health organization, Director of Staff Development and Training, and an Executive Director of several Residential Treatment Centers, and Therapeutic Boarding Schools for both male and female adolescents. Angie also holds a national certification as a Master SAMA Facilitator (Satori Alternative to Managing Aggression), and prides herself in teaching others how to safely and respectfully treat children who pose a physical danger to themselves and others while in crisis.

Ms. Fusco recommends asking the following series of questions when seeking professional placement for an adolescent.

An Educational Consultant is a skilled professional who provides counseling and advice to parents about choosing an appropriate therapeutic school or program as well as traditional schools and colleges for their child. Educational Consultants should operate independently of any institution with related fees being paid by parents for the needs assessment and recommendations. Because areas of expertise differ greatly, parents should take care to make sure the Educational Consultant specializes in meeting the needs of a therapeutic placement.

Questions to ask when hiring an Educational Consultant:

- How long have you been an educational consultant?
- What is your background?
- What positions (roles) in the Mental Health / Educational Field have you held?
- Do you belong to any professional organizations, and how do you keep up with information and trends in the field?
- If you belong to a professional organization for Educational Consultants, can you share a copy

with me of the ethical standards you are required to adhere to?

- What services do you offer for families and children in need?
- What is your role when working with children and families?
- What is your relationship with the schools and programs you work with, and do you ever accept compensation for a referral?
- How much communication can we expect from you if we sign a contract? How will communication take place? (emails, phone calls, Zoom calls)
- What will your role be with our child, our family and the school or program once he/she has been placed?
- Can you provide references of other families you have worked with?

Wilderness Therapy Program: A specialized outdoor experience that assesses and more clearly diagnoses issues and deals with behavioral issues, leading to recommendations for the most optimal setting for continued treatment. It is not an end in and of itself but a tool to help design a course of treatment. Staff include licensed therapists along with support staff who are trained to work in outdoor settings. They are accredited by the OBH and sometimes CARF or JCAHO. Psychiatric services are generally on a contracted basis with a nurse overseeing distribution of medication. Length of stay: 8–12 weeks.

Questions to ask when selecting a Wilderness Program (adapted from www.allkindsoftherapy. com):[139]

- How often will students shower, wash clothes etc.? Ask about the protocols ensuring young adults hygiene.
- What are the meals like? How does the program accommodate special dietary needs?
- How do you deal with a young person/young adult when they are struggling?
- How will your treatment model work with my child (explain your child on their worst day)?
- What is the process for a student who walks away from the program, or a young adult who no longer wants to participate? How often have you had a student run from or be discharged from a program?
- Do you ever have to restrain a student? If so, what would be the circumstances? What method(s) is used for restraint?
- What happens in extreme temperatures? What program changes happen over the winter?
- What happens over the holidays?
- If the program owns a teen wilderness therapy program and a young adult wilderness track, what are the differences?
- Does the program encompass any areas of specialized treatment?
- Does the program exclude any applicants? If

so, what would be the reason(s) for denial for admission to the program?

State Licensing

States that license adolescent (ages 10–18) programs often do not have adult (ages 18+) program licenses. Some states do not have any wilderness therapy regulations. Most reputable wilderness therapy programs follow state licensing requirements anyway. ASK.

Staff

Field staff are out in the field with the student 24/7, usually for eight days. Therapists typically visit the field or base camp two days a week. A majority of student therapeutic work occurs outside of therapist hours. The therapist communicates weekly with the parent or guardian.

Understanding the Milieu (the Therapeutic Environment)

- Where does the program find or hire program staff?
- How long do field instructors (staff) remain at the program?
- Programs expect staff to "live out the model." Read any staff training information provided on the website to gain more insight.
- Programs typically expand in the summer. How does the program staff the larger groups?
- What is the field staff schedule? When field staff

change shifts, what is the protocol?

- What is the process for weeding out staff who cannot hold boundaries with students or are not supporting the process?

Clinical

Wilderness Therapy Programs for young adults often have extremely different models to effect or support change in the student. The key is understanding the therapeutic model and the inherent types of intervention. Equally important is the clinician working with your student.

Do the therapists share groups, or does each therapist have their own group? This will explain the philosophy regarding therapists, how seasoned they are and how the clinical department functions.

- What if I do not like or connect with the therapist?
- How do you handle clients who have had little success with therapists in the past?
- How much time per week will the student have individually with the therapist? How much time in group therapy?
- Which therapist is right for my young adult?
- If my student becomes stuck, apprehensive, or combative, what would the therapist typically do?
- What are the expectations of me as a parent, family member or guardian? (workshops, assignments, webinar participation, etc.)

Residential Treatment Center: A medical setting that is focused first on providing therapy and mental health services as well as basic educational offerings. Basic educational needs are met with a shortened school day due to the demands of the therapeutic services. Staff include licensed therapists and teachers. Psychiatric and nursing services generally on-site. They are accredited by JCAHO or CARF and will have academic accreditation appropriate to a special needs setting. Length of stay: 6–12 months.

Therapeutic Boarding School: A school setting structured much like a traditional boarding school with educational offerings appropriate to the students. They also offer group, individual, and family therapy with the number of sessions varying according to need. TBS are accredited as traditional boarding schools sometimes supplemented by JCAHO or CARF accreditation. Staff include licensed teachers and therapists and support staff with varying degrees. Psychiatric services are generally on a contracted basis with nursing services on-site. Length of stay: 6–18 months.

Questions to ask when selecting a Residential Treatment Center (RTC) or Therapeutic Boarding School:

Licensing and Current Legal Standing

- Is the program/school licensed by the state? If so, what agency? Is the license current and is the program/school in good standing?

- Who is the program/school owned by? Are they for profit or non-profit?
- Has the program/school received any citations from the licensing agency in the past three years?
- If so, what were the citations for and what was the outcome. (This is public record accessed by request through the licensing agency.)
- Has the program/school ever been sued? If so, what was it for?
- Is the program/school accredited by any agencies? If so, which one and is their accreditation current and in good standing?
- Do you do criminal background checks on your staff? How often?

Academic Considerations

- Is the program/school academic curriculum accredited by an agency? If so, which one?
- Do academic credits transfer from state to state?
- Can students get their high school diploma from the program/school? Can students get a GED while at the program/school?
- How do you support students with learning differences?

RTC Programs and Therapeutic Boarding Schools are often composed of multiple divisions headed by a director.

Identify the different divisions such as Executive, Clinical, Medical, Academic, Residential and ask the following questions of each branch:

How long have they been there? What are their credentials and qualifications?

Therapists

- How many therapists are on your staff?
- What is the typical caseload that each therapist carries?
- How often will my child receive individual therapy? Group therapy? Family therapy?
- Do therapists receive continuing education and training concerning new information and trends?

Medical

- Who provides medical services to the residents? What are their qualifications and credentials?
- What happens if my child has a medical or mental health emergency?
- How are resident/student medications monitored and administered?

Clinical

- Do you have an attending psychiatrist? How often does he/she see students? How are medication changes handled by the psychiatrist and school/program?

- Do you work with a psychologist? If so, what is their role within the school/program?
- Does each student have an individualized Master Treatment Plan? How much input do the parents have in the treatment goals and Master Treatment Plan for their child? How often is this plan reviewed and by whom? What is the process for adding or subtracting goals from the Master Treatment Plan? How much input do the parents have in this process?
- Do you have any outcome studies that provide proof of your program's success? Can you provide me with the data from the outcome measures that you track? How do you measure progress within the program?

Residential Staff

- How many residential/program supervisors do you have?
- How are they trained? What is the average length of service among them?
- What is the supervision and staff ratio throughout the day? At night?

Program Details

- What is the admissions process and what is the criteria for student admission?
- What is the average length of stay for your students?
- Does the program work off of a level system? What is the philosophy around the program model?
- What kind of social and recreational activities do you provide for the students? Does the program include opportunities for community service?
- How do you discipline your students? Give an example of a form of discipline that is used at your program? What is the most severe consequence you use at your program?
- How often will I speak to my child?
- How often will I have the chance to see my child?
- What kind of support do you provide for the family?

Financial Considerations

- What are all the costs associated with your school? Are there any costs not accounted for?
- Does insurance cover any costs associated with your school/program? Do you provide superbills for therapy services?
- Is there any financial assistance available to parents?
- Can you provide me with parent references to call?

Get references for parents who currently have a student enrolled at the school/program, as well as references for former parents.

Psychiatric Hospital: Utilized primarily for crisis intervention in cases of serious safety concern. The first line of treatment is to stabilize with medication until further placement can be found. JCAHO accredited. While school activities may be offered, the clients are not there long enough to warrant academic accreditation. Staff include licensed Nurses, Therapists, Social Workers and Psychiatrists with support staff. Length of stay: 1 day–3 weeks.

Special Note: Placement in a psychiatric hospital, with occasional exceptions, is often based on immediate need. The process typically involves a need for rapid stabilization and medication in order to gain the next step. Because of the accelerated time frame in which placement can occur, insurance, available space, and quality of care are at the top of the list of considerations.

Twenty-Seven

The Transport

Identifying the program best suited for your child's needs is a big, important job. Getting them safely and without incident to the program is the bigger job. In my case, my daughter was twelve years old, living at home, and had no idea what was about to happen. She did not have an extensive network of friends that could rescue her from the grips of her parents' plans, nor did she drive or have access to a source of revenue. Furthermore, boarding a plane and arriving in a distant city was still an intimidating proposition, beyond her ability to navigate. It was highly unlikely she would bolt and run. The circumstances I had to work with were simple and straightforward, allowing me to escort my daughter to the front door of the wilderness program's field house.

This is not always the case and sometimes parents find themselves in a position with few options. This is when a transport service may be the best solution.

Allen Cardoza

A licensed private investigator for more than thirty years and the founder of West Shield Adolescent Services, Allen and his staff have escorted over twelve thousand teens to specialized schools and programs throughout the world. In addition, they have located and returned hundreds of runaways and retrieved many abducted children. Mr. Cardoza was an instructor of Non-Violent Crisis Intervention, and is a former president of the World Association of Detectives. Allen's philosophy of transport is that therapeutic escorts and duty of care are always the most important concern. The safety of the adolescent is the cornerstone on which the transport and care of the student is built. His systematic therapeutic approach toward adolescents includes immediately lowering anxiety, gaining trust and reducing fear throughout the transport process.

Mr. Cardoza recommends asking the following series of questions when seeking professional therapeutic transport for an adolescent.

Professional Transport: A Professional Transport Agent is a skilled professional who works closely with both the referring party and parents to safely facilitate students to a therapeutic program. The best transport agents utilize non-violent crisis intervention techniques and employ excellent communication skills to resolve conflicts. Well-trained agents work patiently and compassionately with the student to lower anxiety, build trust, and reduce fear.

Important Questions to Ask a Transport Company:

- How long has the company been in business?
- Are you state licensed? If so, what agency? Is the license current and is the company in good standing? Has the company received any citations from the licensing agency in the past three years?
- If so, what were the citations for and what was the outcome? (This is public record accessed by request through the licensing agency.)
- Has the company ever been sued? If so, what was it for?
- Does your state require background checks on agents? Does the company conduct background checks on agents?
- Do the agents have any special medical training such as CPR, BLS (basic life support)?
- Do your agents work directly for you or are they contract?
- How much professional insurance coverage does your company carry? What type and level of coverage?
- What are your company's policies regarding physical and mechanical restraint?
- Do your agents always work in teams of two and one same-sex agent present?

Twenty-Eight

Safeguarding Kids on the Internet

Safeguarding our kids on the internet is of utmost importance. If you have read to this point in the book, my guess is you agree. Ironically, you can type into almost any search engine "parental controls for . . . *fill in the blank*" and more times than not, produce some type of advice or quick directions regarding your request. It is also possible to query the opposite to undo parental controls. It is a true cat and mouse game at its finest, which leads to the next question: Is your kid smart enough to figure this out? The answer: Absolutely!

Most parental controls function as a **block, limit,** or an **alert**. In other words, a parent can **block** access to certain information on the internet by identifying key words. An obvious example of this would be "sex, porno, and XXX." Slang terms such as "cherry pie, hot chicks, and hot wheels" is another common pathway for access to pornographic material; however, blocking these words may be more problematic. In addition, be aware there are search engines specifically designed to locate pornography for users.

The majority of parental controls have an ability to **limit** screen usage by setting a specific time frame as well as actual time spent on a device. An example might be restricted access from Monday–Friday 9:00 p.m.–6:00 a.m. A parent might also elect to reduce the total amount of data used per day in turn affecting the time spent on devices.

Finally, parental controls can be set to provide notification to parents through an **alert** that a specific app is being accessed in real time. It is still the job of the parent to locate the device in use and physically run a thorough check.

Parental controls do not take the place of consistently involved parents on the ground. These tools will help to prevent, not guarantee an innocent or curious kid from accidentally stumbling upon questionable sites. Having said that, as much as I would like to believe all of my children were born angels, they remain complex individuals with minds of their own, capable of wandering from the designated path.

The world of technology is dynamic and ever-changing, requiring parents to remain vigilant in continually checking their children's online pursuits. In addition, it is advisable to stay up-to-date on software that will help filter and monitor web content as well as retrieve deleted material and history on electronic devices.

FYI: Most modems and routers have built in parental controls. The following companies have detailed information on parental controls on their websites.

Internet Service Providers

- AT&T
- Comcast
- EarthLink
- NetZero
- Sprint/T-Mobile
- Verizon
- Time Warner

Smartphones and Tablets

- Apple
- Android
- Google Play Store

Search Engines

- Bing
- Google Safe Search
- Yahoo

Online Gaming and Consoles

- Fortnite
- Nintendo DS
- Nintendo Wii
- PS5, PS4, PS3, PSP
- Xbox

Operating Systems

- Apple
- Chrome OS
- Windows

Internet Browsers

- Firefox
- Google Chrome
- Internet Explorer
- Safari

Internet Streaming Media Providers

- Amazon Prime Video
- HBO Now
- Hulu
- Netflix
- Philo TV
- Sling TV

Twenty-Nine

The Wooden Sign in the Closet

In my closet, jammed in a tiny space between my shoes and purses, hangs a simple wooden sign that reads, "I hate to spoil the ending, but everything is going to be okay." I began each day of the last four years reading those words and believing one day they would be true.

Today everything is okay, but the elusive truth remains. That being said, there is no definitive end to this story. What makes everything okay is simply the hope of continued steps toward a future filled with promise. The journey is ongoing with many twists and turns, laced with unexpected revelations and boundless opportunity for deeper self-discovery. The presence of tenacity and courage is what lights the path forward.

Not so long ago, my mother shared a letter my daughter had written to her. Enclosed in the letter was a recent picture of my two daughters at the beach sitting on a large rock, arms wrapped around each other like best friends sometimes do. Below the image, she had written in perfect handwriting the following:

> "I've learned that people will forget what you said, people will forget what you did, but people will never forget how you made them feel."[140]—Maya Angelou

Within the power of Angelou's quote lies the tiny glimmer of hope that sustains tomorrow for those who believe . . . and my daughter does believe.

Bibliography

"20 Early Signs to Recognize Online Predators." Online Sense. August 22, 2019. https://onlinesense.org/signs-online-predators/.

"20 Mind-Blowing Stats about the Porn Industry and Its Underage Consumers." Fight the New Drug, Inc. December 4, 2020. https://fightthenewdrug.org/10-porn-stats-that-will-blow-your-mind/#sthash.bECDDFUx.dpbs.

"50 Surprising Social Media Statistics (in 2019)." Mediastreet. April 23, 2019. https://mediastreet.ie/50-surprising-social-media-statistics-in-2019/#:~:text=%2050%20Surprising%20Social%20Media%20Statistics%20%28In%202019%29,lot%20of%20time%20talking%20about%20Facebook%2C...%20More%20.

"Brain Activity in Sex Addiction Mirrors That of Drug Addiction." Neuroscience News. July 11, 2014. https://neurosciencenews.com/psychology-addiction-triggers-neuroimaging-1179/.

"CommScope Research on Gen Z Tech Intimates Reveals an Always-On Mindset." Business Wire. October 16, 2017. https://www.businesswire.com/news/home/20171016005473/en/CommScope-Research-Gen-Tech-Intimates-Reveals-Always-On.

"Enough Is Enough: Impact on the Brain." Enough is Enough. 2021. https://enough.org/stats-impact-on-the-brain.

"Enough Is Enough: Sexual Predators/Exploitation /Child Pornography." Enough Is Enough. Accessed March 29, 2021. https://enough.org/stats_exploitation.

"How the Internet Is Changing Your Brain." Academic Earth. 2021. https://academicearth.org/electives/internet-changing-your-brain/.

"Internet Pornography by the Numbers." Webroot. Accessed April 1, 2021. https://www.webroot.com/us/en/resources/tips-articles/internet-pornography-by-the-numbers.

"Internet Sex Crimes in Texas." Brett A. Podolsky. November 3, 2017. https://brettpodolsky.com/sex-crimes/internet-sex-crimes-in-texas.

"Pornography and Public Health: Research Summary." End Sexual Exploitation. 2019. http://endsexualexploitation.org/wp-content/uploads/NCOSE_Pornography-PublicHealth_Research-Summary_8-2_17_FINAL-with-logo.pdf.

"Pornography Statistics." Family Safe. August 11, 2017. https://www.familysafe.com/pornography-statistics/.

"Social Media and Teens. American Academy of Child and Adolescent Psychology." AACAP. March 2018. https://www.aacap.org/AACAP/Families_and_Youth/Facts_for_Families/FFF-Guide/Social-Media-and-Teens-100.aspx

"TikTok Statistics—Revenue, Users & Engagement Stats [2021]," April 26, 2021, https://influencermarketinghub.com/tiktok-stats/.

"Troubled Teen & Young Adults Therapeutic Programs & Schools." All Kinds of Therapy. All Kinds of Therapy. 2021. http://www.allkindsoftherapy.com/.

"Youth Statistics: Internet & Social Media." ACT for Youth. 2021. http://www.actforyouth.net/adolescence/demographics/internet.cfm.

"YouTube by the Numbers: Stats, Demographics & Fun Facts." Omnicore. January 6, 2021. https://www.omnicoreagency.com/youtube-statistics/.

Bibliography

Alexander, Julia. "YouTube Still Can't Stop Child Predators in Its Comments." The Verge. February 19, 2019. https://www.theverge.com/2019/2/19/18229938/youtube-child-exploitation-recommendation-algorithm-predators.

Allen, Timothy. "Digital Pornography Addiction." Flipsnack. February 25, 2016. https://www.flipsnack.com/Focus/digital-pornography-addiction.html.

Angelou, Maya. "A Quote by Maya Angelou." Goodreads. 2021. https://www.goodreads.com/quotes/5934-i-ve-learned-that-people-will-forget-what-you-said-people.

B., Megan. "How Predators Have Infiltrated Social Media." The Innocent Lives Foundation. April 23, 2019. https://www.innocentlivesfoundation.org/how-predators-have-infiltrated-social-media/.

Bansal, Agam, Chandan Garg, Abhijith Pakhare, and Samiksha Gupta. "Selfies: A Boon or Bane?" *Journal of Family Medicine and Primary Care* 7, no. 4 (2018): 828. https://doi.org/10.4103/jfmpc.jfmpc_109_18.

Bates, Philip. "What Is the Kik App and Why Do Teens Love It?" MUO. October 31, 2019. https://www.makeuseof.com/tag/what-is-kik/.

Baxter, Allison. "How Pornography Harms Children: The Advocate's Role." May 1, 2014. https://www.americanbar.org/groups/public_interest/child_law/resources/child_law_practiceonline/child_law_practice/vol-33/may-2014/how-pornography-harms-children--the-advocate-s-role/#:~:text=Exposure%20to%20pornography%20harms%20children,increasing%20the%20risk%20of%20addiction.

Berry, Deborah. Personal Interview with Allen Cardoza. February 12, 2021.

Berry, Deborah. Personal Interview with Police Lieutenant. February 20, 2021.

Bila, Josephine. "YouTube's Dark Side Could Be Affecting Your Child's Mental Health." Yahoo! Finance. February 13, 2018. https://finance.yahoo.com/news/youtube-apos-dark-side-could-142600188.html.

Brewster, Thomas. "This $1 Billion App Can't 'Kik' Its Huge Child Exploitation Problem." *Forbes*. August 3, 2017. https://www.forbes.com/sites/thomasbrewster/2017/08/03/kik-has-a-massive-child-abuse-problem/.

Burrell, Jackie. "Dangers for Teens and College Kids." *Lifewire*. June 27, 2019. https://www.lifewire.com/.

Campbell, Leah. "Taking Too Many Selfies May Be Bad for Your Teen's Health." Healthline. July 15, 2018. https://www.healthline.com/health-news/taking-too-many-selfies-may-be-bad-for-your-teens-health.

Cashmore, Pete. "Privacy Is Dead, and Social Media Hold Smoking Gun." CNN. October 28, 2009. https://edition.cnn.com/2009/OPINION/10/28/cashmore.online.privacy/.

Chen, Jason. "Finally, Some Actual Stats on Internet Porn." Gizmodo. June 18, 2013. https://gizmodo.com/finally-some-actual-stats-on-internet-porn-5552899.

Chicago Review Press. "CRP's Blog: Screen Schooled Authors Joe Clement and Matt Miles Discuss Technology in the Classroom, What's Really Going on—Think Distracted Kids with Poor Problem-Solving Skills and Little Intellectual Curiosity—and How Parents and Educators Can Counteract It." Blog | *Chicago Review Press*. August 18, 2017. http://www.chicagoreviewpress.com/blog/screen-schooled-authors-joe-clement-and-matt-miles-discuss-technology-in-the-classroom-whats-really-going-on-think-distracted-kids-with-poor-problem-solving-skills-and-little-intelle/.

Cortez, Meghan Bogardus. "21st-Century Classroom Technology Use Is on the Rise (Infographic)." *EdTech Magazine*. September 15, 2020. https://edtechmagazine.com/k12/article/2017/09/classroom-tech-use-rise-infographic.

Davidow, Bill. "Exploiting the Neuroscience of Internet Addiction." *The Atlantic.* July 18, 2012. https://www.theatlantic.com/health/archive/2012/07/exploiting-the-neuroscience-of-internet-addiction/259820/.

Demko, Savannah. "Frequent Internet Use Affects Brain Functioning." Healio. June 11, 2019. https://www.healio.com/news/psychiatry/20190611/frequent-internet-use-affects-brain-functioning.

Dr. Phil. "Dr. Phil's Ten Life Laws." Dr. Phil. July 13, 2003. https://www.drphil.com/advice/dr-phils-ten-life-laws/#:~:text=When%20you%20choose%20the%20behavior%20or%20thought%2C%20you,will%20create%20an%20experience%20of%20alienation%20and%20hostility.

Duke, Rachel B. "'Epidemic' Growth of Net Porn Cited." *Washington Times.* June 15, 2010. https://www.washingtontimes.com/news/2010/jun/15/epidemic-growth-of-net-porn-cited/.

Eadicicco, Lisa. "These Are the Social Media Platforms Teens Are Ditching in 2019." *Business Insider.* July 7, 2019. https://www.businessinsider.com/teens-ditching-facebook-for-youtube-2019-7.

Ehmke, Rachel. "How Using Social Media Affects Teenagers." Child Mind Institute. June 16, 2020. https://childmind.org/article/how-using-social-media-affects-teenagers/#:~:text=How%20Using%20Social%20Media%20Affects%20Teenagers%201%20Indirect,from%20kids%20communicating...%204%20Stalking%20%28and%20being%20ignored%29.

Entmacher, Dan. "Teens and Technology: Pornography Addiction." Dan Entmacher Psychotherapy. September 19, 2017. http://www.danentmacherpsychotherapy.com/teens-technology-pornography-addiction/.

Evon, Dan. "Did Bill Gates, Steve Jobs, and Other Tech Billionaire Parents Advocate Limiting Children's Technology Use?" Snopes.com. August 30, 2018. https://www.snopes.com/fact-check/tech-billionaire-parents-limit/.

Finkelhor, David, and Janis Wolak. "The Aftermath of Sextortion."

National Children's Alliance. February 27, 2018. https://www. nationalchildrensalliance.org/the-aftermath-of-sextortion/.

Foster, B. J. "5 Dangers of Social Media for Teens." All Pro Dad. April 17, 2020. https://www.allprodad.com/5-dangers-of-social-media-for-teens/#:~:text=5%20Dangers%20of%20Social%20 Media%20for%20Teens%201,Video%20Attempts.%205%20 Humiliating%20or%20Publicly%20Shaming%20Others.

———. "Is Your Child Being Damaged by the Selfie Generation?" All Pro Dad. May 22, 2020. https://www.allprodad.com/child-dam-aged-selfie-generation/.

Freed, Richard. "The Tech Industry's Psychological War on Kids." Medium. April 27, 2018. https://medium. com/@richardnfreed/the-tech-industrys-psychologi-cal-war-on-kids-c452870464ce#:~:text=The%20Tech%20 Industry%E2%80%99s%20War%20on%20Kids%201%20 The,...%2010%20The%20Awakening.%20...%20More%20 items.

G., Devan. "67+ Revealing Statistics about Smartphone Usage in 2020." TechJury. October 15, 2020. https://techjury.net/blog/ smartphone-usage-statistics/.

Gordon, Sherri. "How Sexting Really Impacts Teens." Verywell Family. July 20, 2020. https://www.verywellfamily.com/what-are-the-consequences-of-sexting-460557.

Guynn, Jessica. "Facebook Is Addictive and Should Be Regulated like a Cigarette Company: Salesforce CEO." USA Today. January 23, 2018. https://www.usatoday.com/story/tech/ news/2018/01/23/facebook-addictive-and-should-regulat-ed-like-cigarette-company-salesforce-ceo/1059920001/.

Hilton, Donald L. "Pornography Addiction—A Supranormal Stim-ulus Considered in the Context of Neuroplasticity." Socioaffec-tive Neuroscience & Psychology 3, no. 1 (January 2013): 20767–67. https://doi.org/10.3402/snp.v3i0.20767.

Katehakis, Alexandra. "A Quote by Alexandra Katehakis." Goodreads. https://www.goodreads.com/quotes/462905-just-as-a-heroin-addict-chases-a-substance-induced-high-sex.

Keiper, Andrew, and Perry Chiaramonte. "Human Trafficking in America among Worst in World: Report." Fox News. June 23, 2019. https://www.foxnews.com/us/human-trafficking-in-america-among-worst-in-world-report.

Kühn, Simone and Jürgen Gallinat. "Brain Structure and Functional Connectivity Associated with Pornography Consumption: The Brain on Porn." *JAMA Psychiatry* (Chicago, IL) 71, no. 7 (2014): 827–34.

L'Ecuyer, Danielle. "How Social Media Is Directly Affecting Your Mental Health." HealthPrep.com. https://healthprep.com/articles/mental-health/how-social-media-is-directly-affecting-your-mental-health/.

Lee, Bruce Y. "Here Is How Much Sexting Among Teens Has Increased." *Forbes.* September 9, 2018. https://www.forbes.com/sites/brucelee/2018/09/08/here-is-how-much-sexting-among-teens-has-increased/?sh=6eb3b16336f1.

Lee, Dave. "Facebook Founding President Sounds Alarm." BBC News. November 9, 2017. https://www.bbc.com/news/technology-41936791#:~:text=%E2%80%9CGod%20only%20knows%20what%20it's%20doing%20to%20our%20children's%20brains.%E2%80%9D&text=Speaking%20on%20stage%20to%20Mike,%22.

Lustig, Adanya. "Silicon Valley Schools Reject Tech." *Los Altos Town Crier.* January 9, 2019. https://www.losaltosonline.com/news/sections/schools/210-school-features/59216-silicon-valley-schools-reject-tech.

Madigan, Sheri, Anh Ly, Christina L. Rash, Joris Van Ouytsel, and Jeff R. Temple. "Prevalence of Multiple Forms of Sexting Behavior Among Youth." *JAMA Pediatrics* 172, no. 4 (2018): 327. https://doi.org/10.1001/jamapediatrics.2017.5314.

Manning, Jill C. "The Impact of Internet Pornography on Marriage and the Family: A Review of the Research." *Sexual Addiction & Compulsivity* 13, no. 2-3 (2006): 131–65.

McDowell, Josh. *The Porn Epidemic: Facts, Stats and Solutions.* Orlando, FL: Josh McDowell Ministry, 2018.

McGill, Bryant. "A Self Revolution through Love, Intention, and Service." McGill Media. July 19, 2018. https://gomcgill.com/love-is-the-revolution/.

Munnerlyn, Brenda, ed. "How to Identify and Treat Pornography Addiction." Rehab Center. February 4, 2021. https://www.rehab-center.net/treat-pornography-addiction/.

Negash, Sesen, Nicole Van Ness Sheppard, Nathaniel M. Lambert, and Frank D. Fincham. "Trading Later Rewards for Current Pleasure: Pornography Consumption and Delay Discounting." *The Journal of Sex Research* 53, no. 6 (2016): 689–700.

Orlowski, Jeff, Davis Coombie, and Vickie Curtis. *The Social Dilemma.* Transcript. Scraps from the loft. November 30, 2020. https://scrapsfromtheloft.com/2020/10/03/the-social-dilemma-movie-transcript/.

Pantaleon, Katerin. "Facebook Hits 2.8 Billion Users, Revenues Jump by 20%." *Branding in Asia Magazine.* February 18, 2021. https://www.brandinginasia.com/facebook-user-base-hit-2-8-billion-in-2020-revenues-jumped-by-20-yoy/#:~:text=UK-,Facebook%20Hits%202.8%20Billion%20Users%2C%20Revenues%20Jump%20by%2020%25,growth%20for%20the%20American%20company.&text=Earlier%20today%20Facebook%20announced%20they,in%20response%20to%20new%20legislation.

Parker, Wayne. "Why Every Parent Needs to Know about Snapchat." Verywell Family. June 14, 2020. https://www.verywellfamily.com/what-is-snapchat-and-its-use-1270338.

Pilcher, David. "What Silicon Valley Parents Really Think about the Tech They Build for Their Kids." Freeport Press. November 6, 2018. https://freeportpress.com/what-silicon-valley-parents-really-think-about-the-tech-they-build-for-their-kids/.

Pirius, Rebecca. "Texas Sexting Laws for Teens and Minors." www. criminaldefenselawyer.com. October 8, 2020. https://www.criminaldefenselawyer.com/resources/teen-sexting-texas.htm.

Racco, Marilisa. "Is Generation Z Glued to Technology? 'It's Not an Addiction; It's an Extension of Themselves.'" Global News. June 19, 2018. https://globalnews.ca/news/4253835/generation-z-technology-addiction/.

Rudgard, Olivia. "The Tech Moguls Who Invented Social Media Have Banned Their Children from It." Independent. November 6, 2018. https://www.independent.ie/life/family/parenting/the-tech-moguls-who-invented-social-media-have-banned-their-children-from-it-37494367.html.

Rüdiger, Thomas-Gabriel. "The Real World of Sexual Predators and Online Gaming." LinkedIn. December 4, 2017. https://www.linkedin.com/pulse/real-world-sexual-predators-online-gaming-thomas-gabriel-r%C3%BCdiger/.

Savage, Elizabeth Barrett. "Risky 'Sexting': NC Laws Create Felony Conviction Trap for Minors." *Campbell Law Observer*. March 19, 2018. http://campbelllawobserver.com/risky-sexting-nc-laws-create-felony-conviction-trap-for-minors/.

Sehl, Katie. "23 Important TikTok Stats Marketers Need to Know in 2021." Hootsuite. May 5, 2021. https://blog.hootsuite.com/tiktok-stats/.

Silverstein, Jason. "Sex Offenders Are Allowed to Use All Social Media, Supreme Court Rules." *New York Daily News*. April 8, 2018. https://www.nydailynews.com/news/politics/sex-offenders-allowed-social-media-supreme-court-article-1.3260200.

Smith, Rory. "France Bans Smartphones from Schools." CNN. July 31, 2018. https://www.cnn.com/2018/07/31/europe/france-smartphones-school-ban-intl/index.html.

Soucinek, Jason, and Walt Mueller. "What's the Big Deal with Pornography!?!" ProjectSix19. June 30, 2020. https://projectsix19.org/whats-the-big-deal-with-pornography/.

Talarico, Lauren. "Human Trafficking Routinely Happens in Plain Sight. Parents Are Missing the Signs." ktvb.com. August 17, 2019. https://www.ktvb.com/article/news/crime/human-trafficking-routinely-happens-in-plain-sight-parents-are-missing-the-signs/285-5654ad89-3f4d-4a35-b994-9b1222416356.

Theoharis, Mark. "Teen Sexting," www.criminaldefenselawyer.com. September 8, 2020. https://www.criminaldefenselawyer.com/crime-penalties/juvenile/sexting.htm.

Thompson, Lynn. "Internet Has Put a Spotlight on Sex Addiction." Medical Xpress. August 1, 2017. https://medicalxpress.com/news/2017-08-internet-spotlight-sex-addiction.html.

Tribune News Service. "FBI Reveals Online Secrets of Sexual Predators." *Savannah Morning News*. December 15, 2018. https://www.savannahnow.com/zz/news/20181214/fbi-reveals-online-secrets-of-sexual-predators.

Weller, Chris. "5 Tech Industry Moguls Who Raise Their Kids Nearly Tech-Free." *Business Insider*. February 3, 2018. https://www.businessinsider.in/5-tech-industry-moguls-who-raise-their-kids-nearly-tech-free/articleshow/62771749.cms.

———. "Silicon Valley Parents Are Raising Their Kids Tech-Free — And It Should Be a Red Flag." *Business Insider*. February 18, 2018. https://www.businessinsider.com/silicon-valley-parents-raising-their-kids-tech-free-red-flag-2018-2.

Whigham, Julius. "How Sex Predators, Traffickers Are Adapting to Ever-Evolving Tech to Lure Victims." *Palm Beach Post*. May 25, 2018. https://www.palmbeachpost.com/news/crime--law/how-sex-predators-traffickers-are-adapting-ever-evolving-tech-lure-victims/ZtlWqFYRRKDhzc8sbO4S1L/.

Woods, Amanda. "Louvre Visitors Furious over Time Limit for the 'Mona Lisa.'" *New York Post*. August 15, 2019. https://nypost.com/2019/08/14/louvre-visitors-furious-over-time-limit-for-the-mona-lisa/.

Endnotes

CHAPTER 14: SOCIAL MEDIA AND INTERNET STATISTICS

1. Pete Cashmore, "Privacy Is Dead, and Social Media Hold Smoking Gun," CNN, October 28, 2009, https://edition.cnn.com/2009/OPINION/10/28/cashmore.online.privacy/.

2. The above-mentioned statistics are from "50 Surprising Social Media Statistics (in 2019)," Mediastreet, May 14, 2019, https://mediastreet.ie/50-surprising-social-media-statistics-in-2019/#:~:text=%2050%20Surprising%20Social%20Media%20Statistics%20%20%28In%202019%29%2Clot%20of%20time%20talking%20about%20Facebook%2C...%20More%20.

3. Katie Sehl, "23 Important TikTok Stats Marketers Need to Know in 2021," Hootsuite, May 5, 2021, https://blog.hootsuite.com/tiktok-stats/.

4. "TikTok Statistics—Revenue, Users & Engagement Stats [2021]," April 26, 2021, https://influencermarketinghub.com/tiktok-stats/.

5. "Top 20 TikTok Statistics: Key Facts, Figures & Data [2020]," Mediakix, June 11, 2020, https://mediakix.com/blog/top-tik-tok-statistics-demographics/.

6. "50 Surprising Social Media Statistics (in 2019)."

7. "CommScope Research on Gen Z Tech Intimates Reveals an Always-On Mindset," Business Wire, October 16, 2017, https://www.businesswire.com/news/home/20171016005473/en/CommScope-Research-Gen-Tech-Intimates-Reveals-Always-On.

8. "Youth Statistics: Internet & Social Media," ACT for Youth (Survey 2018), http://www.actforyouth.net/adolescence/demographics/internet.cfm.

9. The first five bullet points come from Asad Butt, "101 Mobile Marketing Statistics and Trends for 2020," January 7, 2021, quoracre-

ative.com/article/mobile-marketing-statistics.

10.   Angela Stringfellow, "50 Mobile Marketing Stats to Know for 2021," Digital Examiner, April 2, 2021, www.digitalexaminer.com/mobile-marketing-statistics/.

11.   Deyan G., "67+ Revealing Smartphone Statistics for 2021," March 26, 2021, https://techjury.net/blog/smartphone-usage-statistics.

12.   Ibid.

13.   Research conducted by Thornin Partnership with Benenson Strategy Group, August 2020.7f031133788.1607630830912.16080682 47513.1608130036388.3&__hssc=208625165.2.1608130036388 &__hsfp=4238489979

14.   Wen-Hsu Lin, et al. (2020), "Exposure to sexually explicit media in early adolescence is related to risky sexual behavior in emerging adulthood," PLoSOne, https://www.ncbi.nlm.nih.gov/pmc/articles/PMC7147756/.

15.   D. Herbenick, T. C. Fu, P. Wright, R. Gradus, J. Bauer, & R. Jones, (2020), "Diverse sexual behaviors and pornography use: Findings from a nationally representative probability survey of Americans aged 18–60 years old," The Journal of Sexual Medicine, https://doi.org/10.1016/j.jsxm.2020.01.013.

16.   "20 Must-Know Stats about the Porn Industry and Its Underage Consumers," May 18, 2021, https://fightthenewdrug.org/10-porn-stats-that-will-blow-your-mind.

17.   W. L. Rostad, et al., "The association between exposure to violent pornography and teen dating violence in grade 10 high school students," Archives of Sexual Behavior (2019), http://doi.org/10.1007/s10508-019-1435-4.

18.   Josh McDowell, "The Porn Phenomenon Study," (2016), https://www.josh.org/resources/apologetics/research/?_ga=2.238048256.1875895857.1623449115-810981249.162344914.

19.   "20 Must-Know Stats about the Porn Industry and Its Underage Consumers," May 18, 2021, https://fightthenewdrug.org/10-porn-

stats-that-will-blow-your-mind.

20. https://www.missingkids.org/gethelpnow/cybertipline

21. https://enough.org/stats_exploitation

22. National Center for Missing and Exploited Children, Exploited Children Statistics. Accessed May 3, 2019, https://enough.org/stats_exploitation.

23. Simone Kühn and Jürgen Gallinat, "Brain Structure and Functional Connectivity Associated With Pornography Consumption," JAMA Psychiatry 71, no. 7 (January 2014): 827–28, https://doi.org/10.1001/jamapsychiatry.2014.93.

24. "Internet Pornography by the Numbers: A Significant Threat to Society," Webroot, accessed April 1, 2018, https://www.webroot.com/us/en/resources/tips-articles/internet-pornography-by-the-numbers.

25. Ibid.

26. Josh McDowell, The Porn Epidemic: Facts, Stats and Solutions (Orlando, FL: Josh McDowell Ministry, 2018), 13, https://www.josh.org/wp-content/uploads/Porn-Epidemic-Executive-Synopsis-9.25.2018.pdf.

27. "Pornography and Public Health: Research Summary," End Sexual Exploitation (2019), http://endsexualexploitation.org/wp-content/uploads/NCOSE_Pornography-PublicHealth_ResearchSummary_8-2_17_FINAL-with-logo.pdf.

28. McDowell, The Porn Epidemic, 13.

29. Peter Wade, "The World Watched a Lot of Porn in 2016," Esquire, January 8, 2017, https://www.esquire.com/lifestyle/news/a52119/pornhub-2016/.

30. McDowell, The Porn Epidemic, 13.

31. Jill C. Manning, "The Impact of Internet Pornography on Marriage and the Family: A Review of the Research," Sexual Addiction & Compulsivity: The Journal of Treatment & Prevention, 13:2–3, 131–65, http://dx.doi.org/10.1080/10720160600870711.

CHAPTER 15: UNDERSTANDING HOW AND WHY SOCIAL MEDIA WAS DESIGNED AND THE PSYCHOLOGY BEHIND IT

32.   Katerin Pantaleon, "Facebook Hits 2.8 Billion Users, Revenues Jump by 20%," Branding in Asia Magazine, February 18, 2021, https://www.brandinginasia.com/facebook-user-base-hit-2-8-billion-in-2020-revenues-jumped-by-20-yoy/#:~:text=UK-,Facebook%20Hits%202.8%20Billion%20Users%2C%20 Revenues%20Jump%20by%2020%25,growth%20for%20the%20 American%20company.&text=Earlier%20today%20Facebook%20 announced%20they,in%20response%20to%20new%20legislatio.

33.   Marilisa Racco, "Is Generation Z Glued to Technology? 'It's Not an Addiction; It's an Extension of Themselves,'" Global News, June 19, 2018, https://globalnews.ca/news/4253835/genera-tion-z-technology-addiction.

34.   The bulk of information in this section regarding the psychology behind social media is from Richard Freed, "The Tech Industry's Psychological War on Kids," Medium, April 27, 2018, https://medium.com/@richardnfreed/the-tech-industrys-psychologi-cal-war-on-kids-c452870464ce#:~:text=The%20Tech%20Indus-try%E2%80%99s%20War%20on%20Kids%201%20The,...%20 10%20The%20Awakening.%20...%20More%20items.

35.   Dave Lee, "Facebook Founding President Sounds Alarm," BBC News, November 9, 2017, https://www.bbc.com/news/tech-nology-41936791#:~:text=%E2%80%9CGod%20only%20 knows%20what%20it's%20doing%20to%20our%20children's%20 brains.%E2%80%9.

36.   Jessica Guynn, "Facebook Is Addictive and Should Be Regu-lated like a Cigarette Company: Salesforce CEO," USA Today, January 23, 2018, https://www.usatoday.com/story/tech/news/2018/01/23/facebook-addictive-and-should-regulat-ed-like-cigarette-company-salesforce-ceo/1059920001/.

37.   Bill Davidow, "Exploiting the Neuroscience of Internet Addiction,"

The Atlantic, July 18, 2012, https://www.theatlantic.com/health/
archive/2012/07/exploiting-the-neuroscience-of-internet-addic-
tion/259820/.

38. Ibid.

CHAPTER 16: HOW TECHNOLOGY IMPACTS THE BRAIN

39. Bryant McGill, "A Self Revolution through Love, Intention, and
Service," McGill Media, July 19, 2018, https://gomcgill.com/
love-is-the-revolution/.

40. Meghan Bogardus Cortez, "21st-Century Classroom Technology
Use Is on the Rise (Infographic)," EdTech Magazine, September
15, 2020, https://edtechmagazine.com/k12/article/2017/09/
classroom-tech-use-rise-infographic.

41. "CRP's Blog: Screen Schooled Authors Joe Clement and Matt
Miles Discuss Technology in the Classroom, What's Really
Going on—Think Distracted Kids with Poor Problem-Solving
Skills and Little Intellectual Curiosity—and How Parents and
Educators Can Counteract It," Blog | Chicago Review Press,
August 18, 2017, http://www.chicagoreviewpress.com/blog/
screen-schooled-authors-joe-clement-and-matt-miles-discuss-tech-
nology-in-the-classroom-whats-really-going-on-think-distracted-
kids-with-poor-problem-solving-skills-and-little-intelle/.

42. Ibid.

43. Savannah Demko, "Frequent Internet Use Affects Brain Functioning," Healio, June 11, 2019, https://www.healio.com/news/psychi-
atry/20190611/frequent-internet-use-affects-brain-functioning.

44. "How the Internet Is Changing Your Brain," Academic Earth
(AcademicEarth.org., 2021), https://academicearth.org/electives/
internet-changing-your-brain/.

45. Danielle L'Ecuyer, "How Social Media Is Directly Affecting Your
Mental Health," HealthPrep, 2020, https://healthprep.com/
articles/mental-health/how-social-media-is-directly-affecting-your-
mental-health/.

46.   Ibid.

47.   Sherri Gordon, "How Social Media Negatively Affects the Teen Brain," Verywell Family, July 13, 2020, https://www.verywellfamily.com/ways-social-media-affects-teen-mental-health-4144769.

48.   Ibid.

49.   Danielle L'Ecuyer, "How Social Media Is Directly Affecting Your Mental Health."

50.   Ibid.

51.   "Statistics:Porn's Impact on the Brain," Enough Is Enough, 2021, https://enough.org/stats-impact-on-the-brain.

52.   Sesen Negash, et al., Journal of Sex Research (2015), https://www.tandfonline.com/doi/full/10.1080/00224499.2015.1025123.

53.   Simone Kühn and Jürgen Gallinat, "Brain Structure and Functional Connectivity Associated with Pornography Consumption," 828.

54.   Lynn Thompson, "Internet Has Put a Spotlight on Sex Addiction," Medical Xpress, August 1, 2017, https://medicalxpress.com/news/2017-08-internet-spotlight-sex-addiction.htm.

CHAPTER 17: ONLINE BEHAVIORS AND ASSOCIATED RISKS

55.   "Dr. Phil's Ten Life Laws," Dr. Phil, July 13, 2003, https://www.drphil.com/advice/dr-phils-ten-life-laws/#:~:text=When%20you%20choose%20the%20behavior%20or%20thought%2C%20you,will%20create%20an%20experience%2.

56.   Bruce Y. Lee, "Here Is How Much Sexting Among Teens Has Increased, Forbes, September 8, 2018, https://www.forbes.com/sites/brucelee/2018/09/08/here-is-how-much-sexting-among-teens-has-increased/?sh=49da19a136f1.

57.   Ibid.

58.   Ibid.

59.   Rachel Ehmke, "How Using Social Media Affects Teenagers," Child Mind Institute, June 16, 2020, https://childmind.org/article/how-using-social-media-affects-teenagers/#:~:text=How%20Using%20Social%20Media%20Affects%20Teenagers%201%20

Indirect,from%20kids%20communicating...%204%20Stalking%20
%28and%20being%20ignored%29.

60. "Social Media and Teens," American Academy of Child and Adolescent Psychiatry, March 2018, https://www.aacap.org/AACAP/Families_and_Youth/Facts_for_Families/FFF-Guide/Social-Media-and-Teens-100.aspx.

61. B. J. Foster, "5 Dangers of Social Media for Teens," All Pro Dad, April 17, 2020, https://www.allprodad.com/5-dangers-of-social-media-for-teens/#:~:text=5%20Dangers%20of%20Social%20Media%20for%20Teens%201,Video%20Attempts.%205%20Humiliating%20or%20Publicly%20Shaming%20Others.

62. AACAP, "Social Media and Teens."

63. Jackie Burrell, "Dangers for Teens and College Kids," Lifewire, June 27, 2019, https://www.lifewire.com/.

64. B. J. Foster, "5 Dangers of Social Media for Teens."

65. Bruce Y. Lee, "Here Is How Much Sexting Among Teens Has Increased."

66. The previous four points are taken from Agam Bansal et al., "Selfies: A Boon or Bane?" Journal of Family Medicine and Primary Care 7, no. 4 (September 4, 2018): 828, https://doi.org/10.4103/jfmpc.jfmpc_109_18.

67. Amanda Woods, "Louvre Visitors Furious over Time Limit for the 'Mona Lisa,'" New York Post, August 14, 2019, https://nypost.com/2019/08/14/louvre-visitors-furious-over-time-limit-for-the-mona-lisa/.

68. Agam Bansal et al., "Selfies: A Boon or Bane?"

69. Leah Campbell, "Taking Too Many Selfies May Be Bad for Your Teen's Health," Healthline, July 5, 2018, https://www.healthline.com/health-news/taking-too-many-selfies-may-be-bad-for-your-teens-health.

70. B. J. Foster, "Is Your Child Being Damaged by the Selfie Generation?" All Pro Dad, May 22, 2020, https://www.allprodad.com/child-damaged-selfie-generation/.

71.   The 2020 statistics are taken from "YouTube by the Numbers: Stats, Demographics & Fun Facts," Omnicore, updated April 2, 2021. https://www.omnicoreagency.com/youtube-statistics/, 1.

72.   Josephine Bila, "YouTube's Dark Side Could Be Affecting Your Child's Mental Health," Yahoo! Finance, February 13, 2018, https://finance.yahoo.com/news/youtube-apos-dark-side-could-142600188.html.

73.   Wayne Parker, "The Dark Side of Snapchat," Verywell Family, June 14, 2020, https://www.verywellfamily.com/what-is-snapchat-and-its-use-1270338.

74.   B. J. Foster, "5 Dangers of Social Media for Teens."

75.   AACAP, "Social Media and Teens," https://www.aacap.org/AACAP/Families_and_Youth/Facts_for_Families/FFF-Guide/Social-Media-and-Teens-100.aspx.

76.   Ibid.

77.   Leah Campbell, "Taking Too Many Selfies May Be Bad for Your Teen's Health."

78.   Agam Bansal et al., "Selfies: A Boon or Bane?"

79.   B. J. Foster, "Is Your Child Being Damaged by the Selfie Generation?"

80.   Rachel Ehmke, "How Using Social Media Affects Teenagers."

CHAPTER 18: TECH GIANTS AND THEIR CHILDREN

81.   Richard Freed, "The Tech Industry's Psychological War on Kids," Medium, April 27, 2017, https://medium.com/@richardnfreed/the-tech-industrys-psychological-war-on-kids-c452870464ce#:~:text=The%20Tech%20Industry%E2%80%99s%20War%20on%20Kids%201%20The,...%2010%20The%20Awakening.%20...%20More%20items.

82.   Chris Weller, "5 Tech Industry Moguls Who Raise Their Kids Nearly Tech-Free," Business Insider, February 3, 2018, https://www.businessinsider.in/5-tech-industry-moguls-who-raise-their-kids-nearly-tech-free/articleshow/62771749.cms.

83. Olivia Rudgard, "The Tech Moguls Who Invented Social Media Have Banned Their Children from It," Independent, November 6, 2018, https://www.independent.ie/life/family/parenting/the-tech-moguls-who-invented-social-media-have-banned-their-children-from-it-37494367.htm.

84. Chris Weller, "5 Tech Industry Moguls Who Raise Their Kids Nearly Tech-Free."

85. Ibid.

86. David Pilcher, "What Silicon Valley Parents Really Think about the Tech They Build for Their Kids," Freeport Press, November 6, 2018, https://freeportpress.com/what-silicon-valley-parents-really-think-about-the-tech-they-build-for-their-kids/.

87. Ibid.

88. Chris Weller, "Silicon Valley Parents Are Raising Their Kids Tech-Free—and It Should Be a Red Flag," Business Insider, February 18, 2018, https://www.businessinsider.com/silicon-valley-parents-raising-their-kids-tech-free-red-flag-2018-2.

89. Ibid.

90. Dan Evon, "Did Bill Gates, Steve Jobs, and Other Tech Billionaire Parents Advocate Limiting Children's Technology Use?" Snopes.com, August 30, 2018, https://www.snopes.com/fact-check/tech-billionaire-parents-limit/.

91. Olivia Rudgard, "The Tech Moguls Who Invented Social Media Have Banned Their Children from It."

92. Dan Evon, "Did Bill Gates, Steve Jobs, and Other Tech Billionaire Parents Advocate Limiting Children's Technology Use?"

93. Adanya Lustig, "Silicon Valley Schools Reject Tech," Los Altos Town Crier, January 9, 2019, https://www.losaltosonline.com/news/sections/schools/210-school-features/59216-silicon-valley-schools-reject-tech.

94. Ibid.

95. Rory Smith, "France Bans Smartphones from Schools," CNN, July 31, 2018, https://www.cnn.com/2018/07/31/europe/france-

smartphones-school-ban-intl/index.html.

96.   David Pilcher, "What Silicon Valley Parents Really Think about the Tech They Build for Their Kids."

97.   Chris Weller, "Silicon Valley Parents Are Raising Their Kids Tech-Free—and It Should Be a Red Flag."

CHAPTER 19: INTERNET PORNOGRAPHY AND SEX ADDICTION

98.   Alexandra Katehakis, "A Quote by Alexandra Katehakis," Goodreads, https://www.goodreads.com/quotes/462905-just-as-a-heroin-addict-chases-a-substance-induced-high-sex.

99.   Timothy Allen, "Digital Pornography Addiction," from Focus on the Family, Flipsnack, February 25, 2016, https://www.flipsnack.com/Focus/digital-pornography-addiction.html.

100.   Brenda Munnerlyn, ed., "How to Identify and Treat Pornography Addiction," Rehabcenter.net, February 4, 2021, https://www.rehabcenter.net/treat-pornography-addiction/.

101.   Allison Baxter, "How Pornography Harms Children: The Advocate's Role," May 1, 2014, https://www.americanbar.org/groups/public_interest/child_law/resources/child_law_practiceonline/child_law_practice/vol-33/may-2014/how-pornography-harms-children--the-advocate-s-role/#:~:text=Exposure%20to%20pornography%20harms%20children,increasing%20the%20risk%20of%20addiction.

102.   Dan Entmacher, "Teens and Technology: Pornography Addiction," Dan Entmacher Psychotherapy, September 19, 2017, http://www.danentmacherpsychotherapy.com/teens-technology-pornography-addiction/.

103.   Paul J. Wright, Robert S. Tokunaga, and Ashley Kraus, "A Meta-Analysis of Pornography Consumption and Actual Acts of Sexual Aggression in General Population Studies," Journal of Communications 66, no. 1 (February 2016):183–205, mentioned in

the article "20 Must-Know Stats about the Porn Industry and Its Underaged Consumers," May 18, 2021, https://fightthenewdrug. org/10-porn-stats-that-will-blow-your-mind/.

104. "20 Must-Know Stats About the Porn Industry and Its Underage Consumers," May 18, 2021, https://fightthenewdrug.org/10-porn-stats-that-will-blow-your-mind.

105. John D. Foubert, PhD, "Facts about Today's Pornography 2020," http://www.johnfoubert.com/is-porn-bad.

106. Donald L. Hilton, "Pornography Addiction—A Supranormal Stimulus Considered in the Context of Neuroplasticity," Socio-affective Neuroscience & Psychology 3, no. 1 (January 2013): pp. 20767–20767, https://doi.org/10.3402/snp.v3i0.20767.

107. Rachel B. Duke, "'Epidemic' Growth of Net Porn Cited," Washington Times, June 15, 2010, https://www.washingtontimes.com/news/2010/jun/15/epidemic-growth-of-net-porn-cited/.

108. Ibid.

109. Timothy Allen, "Digital Pornography Addiction."

110. Ibid.

CHAPTER 20: ONLINE PREDATORS

111. Andrew Keiper and Perry Chiaramonte, "Human Trafficking in America among Worst in World: Report," Fox News, June 23, 2019, https://www.foxnews.com/us/human-trafficking-in-america-among-worst-in-world-report.

112. Ibid.

113. "Enough Is Enough: Sexual Predators/Exploitation /Child Pornography," Enough Is Enough, accessed March 29, 2021, https://enough.org/stats_exploitation.

114. Jason Silverstein, "Sex Offenders Are Allowed to Use All Social Media, Supreme Court Rules," New York Daily News, April 8, 2018, https://www.nydailynews.com/news/politics/sex-offenders-allowed-social-media-supreme-court-article-1.3260200.

115. Lisa Eadicicco, "These Are the Social Media Platforms Teens Are

Ditching in 2019," Business Insider, July 7, 2019, https://www.businessinsider.com/teens-ditching-facebook-for-youtube-2019-7.

116. Megan B., "How Predators Have Infiltrated Social Media," Innocent Lives Foundation, April 23, 2019, https://www.innocentlives-foundation.org/how-predators-have-infiltrated-social-media/.

117. Julia Alexander, "YouTube Still Can't Stop Child Predators in Its Comments," The Verge, February 19, 2019, https://www.theverge.com/2019/2/19/18229938/youtube-child-exploitation-recommendation-algorithm-predators.

118. Ibid.

119. Philip Bates, "What Is the Kik App and Why Do Teens Love It?" MUO, October 31, 2019, https://www.makeuseof.com/tag/what-is-kik/.

120. Thomas Brewster, "This $1 Billion App Can't 'Kik' Its Huge Child Exploitation Problem," Forbes, August 3, 2017, https://www.forbes.com/sites/thomasbrewster/2017/08/03/kik-has-a-massive-child-abuse-problem/.

121. Julius Whigham, "How Sex Predators, Traffickers Are Adapting to Ever-Evolving Tech to Lure Victims," Palm Beach Post, May 25, 2018, https://www.palmbeachpost.com/news/crime--law/how-sex-predators-traffickers-are-adapting-ever-evolving-tech-lure-victims/ZtlWqFYRRKDhzc8sbO4S1L/.

122. Thomas-Gabriel Rüdiger, "The Real World of Sexual Predators and Online Gaming," LinkedIn, December 4, 2017, https://www.linkedin.com/pulse/real-world-sexual-predators-online-gaming-thomas-gabriel-r%C3%BCdiger/.

123. Julius Whigham, "How Sex Predators, Traffickers Are Adapting to Ever-Evolving Tech to Lure Victims."

124. "20 Early Signs to Recognize Online Predators," Online Sense, August 22, 2019, https://onlinesense.org/signs-online-predators/.

125. Information in the section "Reality Check" is from "FBI Reveals Online Secrets of Sexual Predators," Savannah Morning News, December 15, 2018, https://www.savannahnow.com/zz/

news/20181214/fbi-reveals-online-secrets-of-sexual-predators.

126. David Finkelhor and Janis Wolak, "The Aftermath of Sextortion," National Children's Alliance, September 29, 2016, https://www. nationalchildrensalliance.org/the-aftermath-of-sextortion/.

127. Thomas-Gabriel Rüdiger, "The Real World of Sexual Predators and Online Gaming," LinkedIn, December 4, 2017, https://www. linkedin.com/pulse/real-world-sexual-predators-online-gam-ing-thomas-gabriel-r%C3%BCdiger/.

CHAPTER 21: NORTH CAROLINA AND TEXAS: THE INTER-NET, SEXTING, AND THE LAW

128. Elizabeth Barrett Savage, "Risky 'Sexting': NC Laws Create Felony Conviction Trap for Minors," Campbell Law Observer, March 19, 2018, http://campbelllawobserver.com/risky-sexting-nc-laws-cre-ate-felony-conviction-trap-for-minors/.

129. Ibid.

130. Mark Theoharis, "Teen Sexting," www.criminaldefenselawyer.com, September 8, 2020, https://www.criminaldefenselawyer.com/crime-penalties/juvenile/sexting.htm.

131. "Internet Sex Crimes in Texas," Brett A. Podolsky, November 3, 2017, https://brettpodolsky.com/sex-crimes/internet-sex-crimes-in-Texas.

132. Ibid.

133. Rebecca Pirius, "Texas Sexting Laws for Teens and Minors," www. criminaldefenselawyer.com, October 8, 2020, https://www.crimi-naldefenselawyer.com/resources/teen-sexting-texas.htm.

134. Ibid.

CHAPTER 22: REALITY CHECK WITH PRIVATE INVESTIGA-TORS AND LAW ENFORCEMENT

135. Lauren Talarico, "Human Trafficking Routinely Happens in

Plain Sight. Parents Are Missing the Signs," ktvb.com, August 17, 2019, https://www.ktvb.com/article/news/crime/human-trafficking-routinely-happens-in-plain-sight-parents-are-missing-the-signs/285-5654ad89-3f4d-4a35-b994-9b1222416356.

136. Ibid.

137. Deborah Berry, Personal Interview with Allen Cardoza, February 12, 2021.

138. Deborah Berry, Personal Interview with Police Lieutenant, February 20, 2021.

CHAPTER 23: AVOIDING THE TECH TRAP

139. Jeff Orlowski, Davis Coombie, and Vickie Curtis, The Social Dilemma (2020) - Transcript, Scraps from the Loft, November 30, 2020, https://scrapsfromtheloft.com/2020/10/03/the-social-dilemma-movie-transcript/.

CHAPTER 26: THE QUESTIONS TO ASK

140. "Troubled Teen & Young Adults Therapeutic Programs & Schools," All Kinds of Therapy, http://www.allkindsoftherapy.com/.

CHAPTER 29: THE WOODEN SIGN IN THE CLOSET

141. Maya Angelou, "A Quote by Maya Angelou," Goodreads, https://www.goodreads.com/quotes/5934-i-ve-learned-that-people-will-forget-what-you-said-people.

CPSIA information can be obtained
at www.ICGtesting.com
Printed in the USA
LVHW091836210322
713994LV00005B/209